D0106542

This book is dedicated to
Edmund White,
its affectionate godfather

Contents

Illustrations

Acknowledgements

The research in Paris for this book was funded by the Institut Britannique de Paris. I received an enormous amount of help and encouragement during my stays there, and would like to thank: Christophe Campos, Henri Chopin, Jacques Derrida, Albert Dichy, Dr Gaston Ferdière, Pierre Guyotat, Julia Kristeva, Jean-Jacques Pauvert, Mme Fernand Pouey, Paule Thévenin (special thanks) and Edmund White; also the staff at the Bibliothèque de l'Arsenal, Bibliothèque Nationale, Bibliothèque Gaston Baty, Bibliothèque Littéraire Jacques Doucet, Bibliothèque de la Littérature Française Contemporaine, and the Institut Mémoires de L'Édition Contemporaine.

In London, I would like to thank: Malcolm Bowie (who supervised my PhD on Artaud's drawings and recordings), Paul Buck, Philippa Edwards, Jane Giles, Rebekah Lefèvre, Robert McCrum, Deborah Rogers, Tracey Scoffield and Sarah Wilson.

And in Berlin, I would like to thank: Saba Komossa (for inspiration), Chris Mühlenberg, Isobel Schroer and Ingrid Raab.

Part of Chapter 1 of this book originally appeared in *Artforum International*, issue of October 1989, under the title 'A Cinema of Cruelty'. Part of Chapter 5 appeared in *Artforum International* in September 1987, under the title 'A Foundry of the Figure'.

All the translations of Artaud's words in this book are my own.

Stephen Barber, 1992

Introduction

The life and work of Antonin Artaud possess a raw power. Long after his death, Artaud's body of work continues to ricochet strongly through contemporary culture. The facts of Artaud's life are stark and austere. He was a writer whose work extended provocatively but disastrously into many unknown channels. His extreme challenge was rejected by the Surrealist movement in Paris. His most productive work comes only after a sequence of journeys, and a long asylum internment.

Artaud's work keeps coming back in new ways. It metamorphoses, struggling to resist any facile systematization. It is in a state of constant transformation, and proves fertile in all its collisions with the creative works it has encountered, both during Artaud's own lifetime and in the forty-five years since his death. As with the other vital figures who have emerged – in tension – through the French language during the twentieth century, such as Jean Genet and Louis-Ferdinand Céline, Artaud was relentless in his determination to make new images of the human body. His work probes issues of abandonment, confinement and creativity, and produces crucial images of the resuscitation of language and life.

Antonin Artaud was born in Marseilles in 1896 and died in Paris fifty-two years later. His work exists as a strange set of traces. We can discover stubborn and ferocious splinters of a will to create material which, although utterly fragmented, tenaciously persists – in the form of writings, drawings, recordings, and photographic images. Artaud was glacial in his attitude. He was infinitely distant from the people to whom he was closest, and from the cultural and political issues of his time. The residue of his life's trajectory is fierce and volatile. It appears as the burning light of a constellation of dead stars. His work is a painful movement through many silences and journeys. Points of apparently intractible breakdown are twinned with sudden breakthroughs into physical and linguistic intensity.

From a distance, Artaud's life indicates failure and misery. It was a constant refusal of security and illusion. His work compulsively attacks ideas of society, family, religion and the body, with great emphasis and discipline. Artaud suffered nervous torture throughout his life and became a drug addict, undergoing repetitiously unsuccessful detoxification treatments. He worked with but also against the Surrealist movement. He fled France after the catastrophic launch of his longstanding dream for the Theatre of Cruelty – an artistic project which was designed to uproot culture and to burn it back into life, as an act directed against society. And he was arrested during the last of his subsequent journeys, to Ireland in 1937, placed in a strait-jacket and interned in the wartime asylums of France, where he experienced anguish and starvation, then fifty-one electroshock comas.

The most productive phase of Artaud's life begins in May 1946, when he was released from the last of those asylums, Rodez, and travelled back to Paris. His body was ruined, crippled by his treatment over the previous nine years. His emaciated figure stalked the post-war Paris of black-market dealings and recrimination. He surrounded himself with a barrier of isolation, broken only for two exceptional performances, and he developed an attitude of acute resistance to the predominant cultural forces in post-war Paris: Sartre's Existentialism and the emergent Lettrist movement of Isidore Isou. Yet it was also at the start of this last period in Paris that Artaud definitively broke the silence imposed upon him at the time of his arrest in 1937. At the end of Artaud's internment, his work burst forward, returned with sensational impact. It had the visceral force of a language allied and bound to the body with which Artaud worked incessantly over the final twenty-two months, until his death in March 1948.

The course of Artaud's work was fractured from its first to last word, from the initiatory correspondence with Jacques Rivière to the final wild letters to the newspaper *Combat*. Artaud's personal obsessions are exaggerated outrageously, until they are used to confront the French nation and the entire world, via the press and radio. The course of Artaud's life has disruptions embedded in it as though they were its natural supporting structure. He suffered numerous catastrophes and humiliations, notably his expulsion from the Surrealist movement at the end of 1926 – after he had provided much of its innovation and poetic momentum – and also the ban placed upon the transmission of his final recording, *To have done with the judgement of god*, in February 1948. All his attempts to produce experimental film and theatre in the 1920s and 1930s collapsed. Artaud's life sustains itself only through attack, in reaction to failure and humiliation.

Towards its end, this life moves through a sequence of physical actions which attempt to exert discipline upon chance, to motivate spontaneity through fury, and to cut the body down to primary elements: bone, pure will, movement, scream. Artaud produces images of this process which are direct, violent and hallucinatory. They provoke a deep reconsideration of responses to the division between self and body. Artaud's two interventions in the social life of Paris between 1946 and 1948 embody these strategies. His performance at the Vieux-Colombier theatre in January 1947 aimed at an acute exposure in poetic and physical terms. And his last project, the censored recording for radio of November 1947–January 1948, created an aural imagery of screams and denunciations that has a driving and dangerous movement, remaining active even now.

In Artaud's perception, the human body is a wild, flexible but flawed instrument that is still in the process of being forged. The body suffers malicious robberies (by society, family and religion) which leave it fixed and futile, smothered to the point of a terminal incoherence and inexpressivity. Throughout his life, Artaud worked through ideas and images which explore the explosion of that useless body into a deliriously dancing, new body, with an infinite capacity for self-transformation. The body would become a kind of walking tree of will. This imagery recurs throughout Artaud's work, forming the core of an anatomical reconstruction from the material of abject fragmentation. In particular, his drawings of the human face – the only remaining authentic element of the anatomy for Artaud – endeavour to obliterate the body's weaknesses and to return it to a vivid manifestation of turbulent movement and experiential existence. The facial features in his drawings – hard bones and concentrated eyes – challenge and reformulate the visual world through the dynamism of their individual creativity. All Artaud's writings, recordings and images of theatre, film and dance have a similar incisiveness. A multiplicity of means is used to dissect what Artaud saw as the infinite potential of human substance. Throughout its course, his work probes the ground from image to text and back, investigating the unstable borders between them, colliding each element against the other until they have been exhaustively tested.

It is this multiplicity of means at play in Artaud's work which gives it such a fascinating richness and attraction. Artaud was not only a writer, he was also a visual artist, a vocal performer, a dancer, a film actor (thereby providing a rich and abundant iconography), a theatre director and actor, a traveller, a destroyer of languages. These components of Artaud's life cut across each other. Media are stripped of their superficial closure, and open out into each other to produce works of great density and force.

This interpenetration of disciplines has facilitated a great creative use of Artaud's work which is neither an absorption nor an appropriation (though cultural reintegration has also been evident, often in the theatrical field, to damaging and derisory effect). Artaud was persecuted and incarcerated by society, neglected and forgotten in his lifetime. His work, an abrupt unscreening of consciousness, has lacerated and enriched the work of many writers, artists, theatre directors, film-makers, poets and actors over the period since his death. In this sense, Artaud's life has extended itself. At the time of his death it began afresh, in a new way.

The sway of Artaud's influence upon innovative and experimental art has been diverse and far-reaching. It ranges from the visual to the vocal to the theoretical. The fiction of the French avant-garde novelist Pierre Guyotat concerns acts of prostitutional sexuality which constantly expand in scale and number. The language at work in his writing is welded into a headlong, exclamatory rush towards an extreme obscenity which is also utterly pure. In common with Artaud, Guyotat views the act of writing as a raw exudation of physical material, a creative expectoration of deadly substances. The body's spore-like trace is spread across the written page. Writing, for Artaud and for Guyotat, is a physical secretion, both savage and interrogative in its impact; it glances sharply off the body. Both writers speak with blunt desire from the sensory reflexes, against social controls. (Guyotat's novel *Éden, Éden, Éden*, 1970, was censored by the French Ministry of the Interior, and he was subjected to abuse and political attacks.) Writing becomes a disciplined and committed intervention which cracks censorship wide open in all its horror.

The Lettrists Henri Chopin and François Dufrêne have explored the range of the body's noises and circulatory movements, inspired by Artaud's final recordings. Chopin first heard a clandestine copy of *To have done with the judgement of god* at the end of the 1940s. Seeking to document the vocal origins of his body, Chopin had a microphone passed down through his throat in order to record his cries from their 'source'; when the microphone became stuck, he suffered much internal damage. Chopin's work with the Sound Poetry group in France and his magazine *OU* have proved productive in terms of research into the body and its most direct and expressive movement, the cry.

There have been many other valuable experiments based on Artaud's work. The leading German artist Georg Baselitz drew his *Pandemonium* manifestos of 1961–62 – which have been crucial to the 'New Expressionist' and 'New Wild' painters in Berlin – from the furious energy and assault of Artaud's Surrealist manifestos and open letters. Julian Schnabel employed one of Artaud's final self-portraits as a 'ready-made' in his citational large-scale painting, *Starting to Sing: Artaud*, of 1981. Rainer Werner Fassbinder's films project an atmosphere of darkness, blood and shock which is close to the substance of Artaud's own film proposals and scenarios; Fassbinder dedicated his film about identity duplication and social alienation, *Despair*, to Artaud. The Japanese dance style pioneered by Tatsumi Hijikata, 'Butoh', approached Artaud's work with its painfully contorted imagery of the dancing anatomy, steeped in desire. Its violent and erotic manipulations of chance and metamorphosis have a source in Artaud's vocal movements and screams. The dancer Sumako Koseki has said: 'Butoh is Artaud's voice at the end of his life.'[1] There have been many other active homages. The work Artaud undertook has assisted in the creation of some of the most sensationally beautiful and original images of fracture and desire produced over the past five decades.

The interaction of Artaud's work with analytical discourse in France also raises the complex, uneasy relationship of that work with psychiatry and psychoanalysis. Philosophers such as Jacques Derrida, Julia Kristeva and Gilles Deleuze have addressed again and again the rhythmic movement and many voices of Artaud's language, with its break from fixed and inflexible modes of expression. Derrida's engagement with Artaud's texts, images and recordings has persisted since the mid-1960s. In his first two essays on Artaud, 'The Stolen Word' and 'The Closure of Representation',[2] he examines the struggle between loss and reduction in Artaud's texts. Language is used as a weapon to counter its own losses and those of the body which drives it; it becomes denser, more aggressively vocal. Representation is a repetitious and malicious process (explicitly social for Artaud) which diverts the immediacy and tangibility of the creative work, so representation is always attacked and opposed. Derrida asserts that representation is fatal and unstoppable in the way it nullifies a text. What he does not point out is that Artaud often *needs* representation to resuscitate his language when it becomes clogged or jammed, and also as raw material upon which to construct violent resurgences from silence. More recently, in a large catalogue of Artaud's drawings published in 1986,[3] Derrida probed the layering of Artaud's visual images. A treacherous layer is countered by a pulverizing attack exerted by Artaud, aimed with clumsy, un-artistic precision at and into the surface of the work. Derrida stresses that the aesthetic object is refused and precluded in Artaud's visual imagery.

Julia Kristeva's essay 'The Subject on Trial'[4] (1977) examines the negativity of Artaud's last work. Artaud's language, propelled by rejection, has an immensely flexible force of meaning through the shattering of its own structures. For Kristeva, the text becomes valuably multiple and expressive, rather than lost, in this process. She writes of the acute compression of Artaud's gestural and oral refusal of society, and uses his February 1947 letter to the Surrealists' leader André Breton to argue that when rejection (which, as Artaud emphasizes in the letter, must always be personal) is given a permanently renewed target in society, then this will lead to one of the great revolutionary 'collective furies' of history, where society and art are at their extreme point of creative collision.

Artaud's last recording, *To have done with the judgement of god*, is philosophically swallowed alive by Gilles Deleuze and Félix Guattari's exuberant and distorting book *A Thousand Plateaus* (1980). In their speculations about the 'body without organs' (a phrase from the recording, where Artaud demands that his new body should be organ-less and immortal), Deleuze and Guattari find their 'question of life and death' in the image of a movement of constant desire, which relentlessly opposes all systematic organization. The vital observation they make is that even in its most dense form, the 'body without organs' and the language used to project it may multiply themselves wildly and cancerously, in a parallel way to industry, money, and the social state. For Deleuze and Guattari, it is these proliferations which are so eruptively and dangerously productive in Artaud's work.

All these writings have an implicit or explicit concern with the various definitions of madness applied to Artaud. The last phase of

Artaud's work, in particular, has suffered from a certain marginalization. It is the work of a man newly released from nine years in five successive asylums, and has sometimes been dismissed summarily. But this last work is far from a psychosis-induced linguistic stalling. More than any other phase of Artaud's work, that from the period after his release from Rodez conveys a magnificent lucidity and lust for life. Utterly stubborn in its torrent of invective and denunciation, it is immensely versatile in terms of its imagery of the body, and in its linguistic experiments.

Artaud's work is always extremely conscious, intentional and wilful. This is one of the reasons why Artaud broke with André Breton's Surrealism in the period leading up to 1926. It had been Breton, along with Philippe Soupault, who had produced the first example of 'automatic writing', *The Magnetic Fields*, in 1919. The process of writing, for Breton and Soupault, was left as far as possible to unconscious reflexes, and was subject to the suggestive juxtapositions of dream imagery. By contrast, the intention to lose control in life, to step back to survey the damage, then to probe the entire process and its results, is strongly present in Artaud's writings. The relinquishment of any kind of control during the actual act of writing – even for the magical eruptions from the unconscious mind which Breton advocated – is relentlessly condemned. Artaud feared sleep, unconsciousness, drunkenness – states where control was lost, where a void might appear.

The sense of self-control is what is so fascinating about Artaud's approach to mental collapse. Madness becomes raw material to be treated with great irony and with great anger. The symptoms of schizophrenia, delirium and paranoia are viewed, assessed and incorporated into Artaud's language. He pre-empts and negates the psychiatric profession's view of his virulent attacks upon society. Psychiatry is an explicitly malicious institution for Artaud. In his recording *To have done with the judgement of god*, he reconstructs a dialogue between himself and the chief psychiatrist at Rodez, Dr Gaston Ferdière:

– You are delirious, Monsieur Artaud. You are mad.
– I am not delirious. I am not mad.

Artaud's approach to madness is manipulative in the extreme. It condenses psychiatric diagnoses and jargon into a flaccid rationale which can then be used to provide its own refutation, executed by Artaud with precision and assertive power. Too great a degree of agility and destructive delight exists in Artaud's demolition of psychiatry for his work to be dismissed as a 'délire de revendication' (the French term introduced by Doctors Sérieux and Capgras for the language of a psychotic patient who reorganizes the world according to his own obsessed and fixated system). This kind of dismissal is what Sigmund Freud and Jacques Lacan undertook, albeit with a certain admiration, in order to theorize and reinforce their position around the writings of Judge Schreber (Freud and Lacan) and 'Aimée' (Lacan). Artaud's total refusal of psychiatrically formulated madness is also an intense questioning of its constitution. With self-probing intricacy, Artaud's refusal undermines and unscreens notions of psychosis. It blatantly *uses* madness, puts madness to work, to take apart its social structure and to produce a transmissible language from that process of disassembly. In Artaud's final recording, this refusal of psychiatry probes and also screams.

Artaud's breakdown in 1937 and subsequent incarceration are always presented by him as a shattering. He was about to speak, to announce imminent transformations on physical, sexual and social levels – but was then silenced and suppressed. He presents his asylum internment as part of a malicious chain of suppressions which extends back from the police, doctors and administrative bodies who were directly involved in his arrest, to the theological, familial and political bodies which upheld it, and through which the concept of madness had its origin. It is this special sensitivity of Artaud's writings towards a pervasive social complicity in individual repression which attracted 'anti-psychiatrists' such as David Cooper and R. D. Laing to them in the 1960s. Artaud's reconstruction of the life of Vincent Van Gogh as a parallel to his own is the crucial material which tries to give authenticity to his imagery of social murders and social suicides.

Above all, Artaud denounced the brutality of psychiatry as it was practised in the 1930s and 1940s, especially the fifty-one electroshock treatments to which he was subjected by Dr Ferdière at Rodez. This denunciation has proved fertile for the Lettrist movement in Paris. Its leader, Isidore Isou, was also a patient of Ferdière following Isou's enthusiastic participation in the May 1968 events in Paris. Isou, together with another Lettrist, Maurice Lemaître, wrote a fiercely polemical book, *Antonin Artaud Tortured by the Psychiatrists* (1970), which – among a swarm of outrageous insults – accuses the 'Nazi-psychiatrist' Ferdière of being a pornographer and drug addict, and 'one of the greatest criminals in the entire history of humanity, a new Eichmann'.[5] Isou and Lemaître's aim is not entirely gratuitous provocation; they also propose a new science of the mind to supersede psychoanalysis, called 'Psychokladology' – this science would employ every branch of scientific and poetic knowledge to combat individual alienation and fragmentation of the self. For Artaud, however, fragmentation is not to be combated – it is itself a weapon, with which to attack and dismantle social systems and languages, and by which the body operates a reclamation of the silenced self.

This dismantling, and the interpenetration of creative and analytical writing, is reminiscent of Jacques Lacan's work. Some connections (notably, the concern with disunity and multiplicity, and the conflict between surface and interior) are evident between the works of Artaud and Lacan. But, in the contact they had during the period 1938–9, the two men were unambiguously hostile. Artaud was at that time an inmate of the Henri-Rousselle clinic at the Sainte-Anne asylum in Paris, where Lacan was in charge of diagnosing patients and arranging for their transfer to other hospitals. Artaud's close friend Roger Blin (who later directed the plays which made Samuel Beckett and Jean Genet internationally famous) went to see Lacan to discuss Artaud's treatment with him. Lacan told Blin that Artaud's case did not interest him, that Artaud was 'fixed'[6] and that he would live to be eighty, but would never write another line. In fact, Artaud barely lived to be fifty, and in his remaining ten prolific years produced several times the amount of work than in his life up to the internment period. In later years, Lacan would warn his followers and students against 'inflaming themselves' in Artaud's manner; if they did display such passion, they should be 'calmed down'.[7] Artaud was unequivocally contemptuous of his treatment at Sainte-Anne. He claimed to have been held in solitary confinement there, silenced and even systematically poisoned. Since no precise diagnosis was made about his condition at Sainte-Anne (beyond that he was chronically and incurably insane), Artaud was sent to the huge asylum of Ville-Évrard, in the eastern suburbs of Paris. During his stay there he was constantly transferred between wards, from the maniacs' ward to the epileptics' ward, from the cripples' ward to the undesirables' ward. The work produced after Artaud's release from internment is insurgent – it breaks silence, and screams against psychiatric medicine, profoundly questioning its basis.

Though Artaud was born in the south of France, in the huge Mediterranean port and linguistic crucible of Marseilles, his life was bound to Paris. His journeys and internments all involved an ultimate return to Paris, undertaken with both attraction and resistance. The areas of Paris most evocative of Artaud's presence are the boulevard du Montparnasse in the 1920s and 1930s, and the boulevard Saint Germain in the final period of 1946–8. Many of his writings were produced in the great literary cafés – the Flore, the Coupole, the Dôme – which formed the core of a particularly gregarious milieu that no longer exists in Paris. Even in the self-imposed solitude of his final Paris period, Artaud spent many of his nights writing in the Saint Germain-des-Prés cafés – sometimes alone, and hostile to interruption, but often in the company of his small group of friends, including Roger Blin and the writer Arthur Adamov. The names of Parisian districts and streets are pervasive in Artaud's later texts, strategically displaced where necessary. *Van Gogh the Suicide of society* ends with the evocation of a huge rock blown from a volcano (an image for Artaud's own body), which lands at the junction of the boulevard de la Madeleine and the rue des Mathurins, two streets which do not geographically intersect. Artaud's relationship with Paris was disruptive and confrontational. Both in his writings and performances, he attacked and enlivened the city in which his work was published and witnessed. At the end of his life, Artaud came to an uneasy compromise with Paris, living in a convalescent home on its outskirts, at Ivry-sur-Seine. Maintaining a cold distance from the literary and social worlds which he believed had enmeshed and rejected him in the 1930s, Artaud was nevertheless positioned for regular denunciatory incursions into the city's life.

Although, in general, Artaud manifested extreme hostility towards his contemporaries, he lived through periods of great artistic productivity and experimentation in Paris: the 1920s with Surrealism, and the period 1946–8 with its many artistic and philosophical movements that emerged in part from the excitement of the liberation from Nazi occupation in 1944. Artaud came into close proximity with many of the greatest artists and writers of the twentieth century: Pablo Picasso, Georges Braque, André Gide, André Breton, Tristan Tzara, Jean Cocteau, Georges Bataille, among others. Occasionally, valuable collaborations resulted from these contacts, not least in the field of interaction between the text and the image. But Artaud could be summarily dismissive of his

famous contemporaries. His friend Jacques Prevel reports that
Artaud 'abominated' Jean-Paul Sartre.[8] And he seems to have taken
no notice whatsoever of the work of either Jean Genet (active in
Paris during Artaud's last period there, but probably stigmatized in
Artaud's perception through his association with Sartre), nor ·of
Louis-Ferdinand Céline, despite the fact that they shared the same
young and adventurous publisher, Robert Denoël, for both of their
first full-scale works, Artaud's biography of the Roman Emperor
Heliogabalus (1934) and Céline's *Journey to the End of the Night*
(1932).

Artaud receptively experienced wild and strange times in his life,
and his work underwent the seismic shudders of a multiple cultural
revolution in terms of the text, the body and the machine. But
Artaud could also abdicate from world events, and exile himself
into the interior impulses of his own body and his creative activities. He lived through both world wars, the first (from the age of
eighteen to twenty-two) partly as a sanatorium patient and partly as
a somnambulistic soldier, the second (from the age of forty-three to
forty-nine) entirely as a mental hospital patient. He participated in
no social or military conflicts, and wrote in response to a newspaper
questionnaire about the Moroccan war of 1925: 'The war, that of
Morocco or any other, appears to me as exclusively a question of
flesh.'[9] During the same period, his disagreement with Breton over
the Surrealist movement's affiliation to the French Communist
Party was motivated largely by their divergence of response to the
term 'revolution'. For Artaud, the contents of the unconscious
mind could never be applied to political and social arenas without,
firstly, a drastic anatomical transformation. All Artaud's rapports
with social and cultural institutions were disrupted by this preoc-
cupying imagery of an individual human body in a process of
grinding metamorphosis. In Artaud's writings, culture and nature
are amalgamated, crushed and brought down to a zero point. They
are subjugated to a physical activity which must be set into movement before any other living structure may exist. The body comes
before the word, and before the world.

Artaud's life was great tragedy – terrible failure upon failure,
suppression after suppression. But he possessed a magisterial and
monumental capacity for reactivation and reinvention. After each
catastrophe, his tenacious proposals for the gestural life of the body
were overhauled and presented in an entirely new way. His Surrealist work of the 1920s attempted experiments on consciousness

through cinematic and poetic work. After the collapse of Artaud's projects for Surrealism, his work re-evolved into the theatrical space. There, the body's tightly controlled and expansively exaggerated gestures, in theatrical performance, aimed to seize the potential for an overwhelming expressivity, using an imagery of blood, disease, death and fire. Once that option had been closed to Artaud by the constraints of the 1930s Parisian theatre, he initiated his great creative journeys, making Mexico and Ireland the sites for an exploration of destructive rituals centred on the body. The first journey ended in disillusionment, and the second in asylum internment.

The final resurgence of Artaud's life, with his release from Rodez, produced an enormous and diverse amount of work. It crossed the borders between disciplines, with the result that a great body of provocative and challenging material was created. The last period is an intensification of all Artaud's previous production. It has a final clarity which is both controlled and feral. The trajectory of Artaud's life and work, including the Theatre of Cruelty proposals and the Surrealist writings, cannot be fully understood without its final perspective and its impact of elucidation. This last work varies from public performances, to recordings which were intended for radio transmission, to texts which were published in mass-circulation newspapers. Artaud's theatrical manifestos of the 1930s, in their collected form, have been subject to numerous critical recuperations which have, to some extent, diminished their virulence. The last work, by contrast, is dispersed and largely unknown: it demands rediscovery.

The life and work of Antonin Artaud interrogate the role of the fragmented but transforming body, in art, literature and performance – within chance and necessity, within damage and reconstitution. The lucid and challenging body-in-movement which Artaud projected remains a figure emphasizing regeneration and the reassertion of liberty. It is an inspiration for whoever now makes new and vital images of the human body, against what Artaud saw as its fearful, static sickness.

I

Surrealism and the Void

Antoine Marie Joseph Artaud was born at eight in the morning of 4 September 1896, at 15 rue du Jardin des Plantes, near the Marseilles zoo. The rue du Jardin des Plantes has since been renamed the rue des trois Frères Carasso. Artaud himself, on many occasions, was to change and distort the name under which he was baptised into the Roman Catholic Church. He adopted numerous pseudonyms, such as Eno Dailor for some of his early Surrealist texts. Before his journey to Ireland in 1937, he styled himself 'The Revealed One' in his prophetic book *The New Revelations of Being*. During the same period, he declared: 'My name must disappear',[1] and he answered to no name at all for the first period of his asylum internment. At the asylum of Ville-Évrard, he adopted his mother's maiden name and asserted that his name was Antonin Nalpas. After his release from the asylums and his return to Paris in 1946, Artaud took for himself the nickname 'le Mômo' (Marseilles slang for a fool or village idiot), and he also distorted his surname to 'outo' and 'Totaud'. Finally, he came to terms with having a name derived from his father's, Antoine Roi Artaud (Antonin is a diminutive, 'little Anthony'). In his last writings, he was able to weld his name, which he felt he had ultimately won for himself, to imagery of an explosive identity:

> Who am I?
> Where do I come from?
> I am Antonin Artaud
> and I say this
> as I know how to say this
> immediately
> you will see my present body
> burst into fragments
> and remake itself
> under ten thousand notorious aspects
> a new body
> where you will
> never forget me.[2]

Artaud's family origins were dispersed across the Mediterranean, from France to Greece and Turkey. His childhood in the great European-African-Asian trading port of Marseilles exposed him to a fertile crisscrossing of languages, dialects and gestural signs which resonate in his multilingual texts. His father ran a shipping company until its financial collapse in 1909, and was often absent on trading journeys during Artaud's childhood; he died in 1924 when Artaud was twenty-seven years old and on the point of adhering to the Surrealist group. His mother, a Levantine Greek, had a great number of children of whom only Artaud, one sister and one brother survived infancy; she died in 1952, having outlived her first child, Antonin. The family atmosphere was deeply restrictive, heated and religious. In family photographs Antonin appears bewildered. Later in life, from his time at the asylum of Rodez until his death, he elaborated an alternative, oppositional family, entirely female, which he called his 'daughters of the heart to be born'. This sexually charged grouping was composed both from imaginary elements and from women Artaud had known during the course of his life. The only members of his actual family to be included were his beloved and sympathetic grandmothers Catherine and Neneka, who had been sisters. As Artaud's 'daughters', they were genealogically inverted from their familial position, to be reborn as Artaud's courageous, erotic warrior-children.

At the age of four years, Antonin had a severe attack of meningitis. The family and their doctor assumed it was due to the child having fallen on his head, and he was not expected to survive. The virus gave Antonin a nervous, irritable temperament throughout adolescence. He also suffered from neuralgia and stammering. His school years in Marseilles were consequently difficult and unsuccessful. At the age of seventeen he underwent a crisis of depression, causing him to burn the poetry which he had been writing for around four years, and to abandon school before taking the leaving certificate, the *baccalauréat*. During his time at Rodez in the 1940s, when Artaud was systematically reinventing his past life, he often wrote of an episode from this period, in which he had been stabbed in the back by a pimp outside a church in Marseilles. At Rodez, he claimed that the attack was the manifestation of a malicious social and religious will, and that he still had a scar from the stab wound. If the narrated event relates to an actual event, it seems likely to have been the result of an altercation between a hoodlum in that violent city and an inexperienced youth looking for

sexual or narcotic adventure. Shortly afterwards, Artaud's parents
arranged for the first in a long series of sanatorium stays for their
disruptive son.

These private 'rest cures' were both prolonged and expensive.
They lasted five years, with a break of two months, June and July
1916, when Artaud was conscripted into the army. He spent his
brief army career with an infantry regiment stationed at Digne, in
the south of France, and was discharged due to his self-induced
habit of sleepwalking. The sanatorium stays were then resumed,
taking the form of a kind of bourgeois internment of the 'difficult'
son. They prefigure the longer and more gruelling internments of
1937–46. The writer Pierre Guyotat wrote of these first internments
that Artaud's family 'had him locked up for simple "troubles" due
to the force of his thought'. Certainly, Artaud wasted no time
during this luxurious incarceration. He was occupied with reading
Rimbaud, Baudelaire and Poe. At the last sanatorium, at Neuchâtel
in Switzerland, Artaud did a great amount of drawing and painting.
Photographs from the period show a morose but attractive young
man with flowing dark hair, adopting intricate and theatrical post-
ures with obvious involvement. In May 1919 the director of the
sanatorium, Dr Dardel, prescribed opium for Artaud, precipitating
a lifelong addiction to that and other drugs. At the end of 1919,
Artaud formulated the project of travelling to Paris in order to
attempt a career in literature, film and theatre. His parents, in
desperation, assented; Dr Dardel arranged for Artaud to be transferred into the care of a colleague in Paris, Dr Toulouse, who was
engaged in a study and categorization of artistic genius. In March
1920, at the age of twenty-three, Artaud made his first independent
journey, to Paris.

The Paris in which Artaud spent his first few creative years
witnessed the flaring-up and subsequent self-willed disintegration
of Dada, the disordered anti-art movement which had its origins in
Zurich and Berlin during World War One. It had converged on
Paris at the end of the war, led by Tristan Tzara. Dada made an
initial alliance with the nascent Surrealist group of André Breton,
which was involved with developing a chance poetry of the
unconscious mind. Artaud was aware of the early Surrealist magazine *Littérature*. Over the three years from his arrival in Paris, the
Surrealist and Dada groups would move into bitter and often
violent confrontation, with Breton eventually assuming an
authoritarian control over the raging momentum which Dada had

generated. The Dada leader, Tristan Tzara, would become a Marxist in the mid-1930s, and would continue to berate the Surrealists for their political vacillations. While Breton channelled the turmoil of Dada and began formulating manifestos for the Surrealist movement out of material fluctuating between automatism, idealism and obsession, Artaud pursued an erratic career as a theatre actor and art critic. Dr Toulouse had given Artaud the co-editorship of his part-artistic, part-scientific periodical *Demain*, and it was in that capacity that Artaud began to develop the critical power which would still be at work twenty-five years later, when he wrote his texts on Van Gogh, Coleridge and Lautréamont. Toulouse was the head psychiatrist at the Villejuif asylum in south-east Paris, where he was pioneering humane treatments for his patients. For his first six months in Paris, Artaud lodged with the Toulouse family. He then began to live an itinerant life, mostly within the eighth and ninth *arrondissements* (districts) of Paris, moving rapidly between cheap hotel rooms, occasionally destitute and dependent upon friends for a place to sleep. This restlessness would continue throughout Artaud's life in Paris, until his departure for Ireland in 1937. It was only during his final period in Paris, from 1946 to 1948, that Artaud found a stable home and working space, at his pavilion in the convalescence clinic at Ivry-sur-Seine.

It was one of Artaud's original intentions to become a successful film actor. His cousin, Louis Nalpas, was one of the leading producers of French commercial cinema during the 1920s and 1930s. But before Nalpas would give him film roles, Artaud needed to obtain some acting experience, and so he turned to the theatre. For four years, and in numerous roles and companies, he acted in the Paris theatre. He usually played minor parts, but attracted considerable attention through the exaggerated, gestural acting style which he developed during this period. A factor in the anti-naturalistic expressivity of this stage technique was Artaud's seeing a performance by a troupe of Cambodian dancers at the Marseilles Colonial Exhibition in June 1922, during a visit to his parents. This experience prefigured the great impact which a performance by Balinese dancers exerted on his proposal for the Theatre of Cruelty, nine years later. Of the many productions in which Artaud acted, certainly the most exceptional was that of Sophocles' *Antigone* in December 1922. This version, directed by Charles Dullin at the Atelier theatre in Montmartre, was adapted by Jean Cocteau and condensed to thirty minutes; the sets were by Pablo Picasso, the

costumes by Coco Chanel, and the music by Arthur Honegger. It
was a great success, despite a demonstration on the opening night
by the Surrealists, who despised Cocteau for his contacts with
Parisian high society. Artaud had the part of Tiresias, and Antigone
was played by a strange but compellingly beautiful young
Romanian actress named Génica Athanasiou.

It was with Génica Athanasiou, in 1922, that Artaud had his first
serious, and sexual, relationship. Previously he had formed
attachments to the sickly, tubercular girls he had met during his
sanatorium years. Génica, however, was robustly attractive, with a
dark complexion (her family originated in Albania). During this
period Artaud was himself alarmingly beautiful, with dark eyes,
prominent cheekbones, and lips stained purple by the laudanum he
had begun to take. A great passion developed between the two
colleagues in Dullin's theatre company; Artaud was twenty-five and
Génica twenty-three. Artaud's letters to Génica Athanasiou
demonstrate an enveloping, wild adoration. He projects their
relationship on to global, even infinite levels, while his response to
the sexual charge of their liaison is more guarded. (Later in life, at
Rodez, he would write of being 'de-virginalized by Génica'.[3])
Génica's own passion was apparently more reserved; she was
ambitious, and it may have been that the attraction she felt for
Artaud was ultimately aimed towards his film-producer cousin. For
the first two or three years they were content. When Artaud had to
return temporarily to his parents in July 1923, through lack of
money, Génica went to stay nearby and they met secretly. But their
acting careers were not progressing well. Génica's strong accent and
her mediocre command of French limited the number of roles she
could take; similarly, Artaud's acting style alienated him from even
some of the more adventurous and amenable theatre directors, such
as Dullin. But the crucial flaw in their relationship was Artaud's
growing drug addiction. Génica was looking for a successful,
metropolitan career and a café-based social life; she became
exasperated with Artaud's increasing dependence on opium and his
futile, unsupervised attempts at detoxification. Their letters
agonize relentlessly over the problem. Artaud wrote: 'I have need of
angels. Enough hell has swallowed me for too many years. But
finally understand this – I have burned up one hundred thousand
human lives already, from the strength of my pain.'[4]

Though the relationship lasted for six years, until 1928, it
became more difficult with each failed drug-withdrawal and

subsequent reproach from Génica. They each had outside affairs, Génica with another actor from Dullin's company, and Artaud with Janine Kahn, who later married the writer Raymond Queneau. Towards the end of their relationship, Artaud wrote to Génica: 'When you have managed to penetrate a certain kind of hatred, it's then that you truly feel love.'⁵ In 1924, Génica began a minor career in the silent cinema. She appears in the Surrealist film *The Seashell and the Clergyman*, taken from a scenario by Artaud, and also in films by G. W. Pabst and Jean Grémillon. Finally, in 1928, Génica left Artaud for Grémillon. Artaud felt 'multiply alone', and continued to write to Génica until 1940, when he was interned at the asylum of Ville-Évrard. He pleaded for heroin and declared: 'Génica, we must leave this world, but for that, the Reign of the Other World must arrive, and I need many armed soldiers . . .'⁶ With the exception of his 'daughters of the heart', Génica Athanasiou was the most important woman in Artaud's life. Even after his release from Rodez in May 1946, he tried unsuccessfully to locate her at an address in the rue de Clignancourt where she had been living in poverty, her acting career having utterly collapsed.

During the latter part of Artaud's theatre acting, towards 1923–4, his writing developed from art criticism and conventionally structured poetry to a mobile substance of extraordinary self-exposition and incision. It was a time of great flux in his life. The initial ecstasy of his relationship with Génica Athanasiou was being submerged in his anxiety over his drug intake, and over the voids and fractures which he perceived in his emergent poetry. He was beginning to be able to publish his work: his first book, *Backgammon of Heaven*, a collection of early poems, was published in May 1923 by the gallery owner Daniel-Henri Kahnweiler, in an edition of 112 copies. Later in life, Artaud rejected this first book and refused to include it in his planned *Collected Works*, claiming that the poems it contained, rhymed and in stanza form, were hopelessly redundant and anachronistic. They had been produced to ingratiate themselves within a particular cultural climate, and that was a source of horror to the Artaud of the 1940s with his uncompromising attitude towards his work and individuality. But in 1923 the publication of his work was a source of great jubilation to him. Artaud also published his own writings in the slight magazine *Bilboquet*, of which he edited and financed the only two issues in February and December 1923. The magazine solely comprised texts by Artaud, and forms a bridge between the art and literary criticism of the kind he had undertaken for Dr Toulouse (and which he would do again for his psychiatrist Dr Ferdière at Rodez), and the raw-nerved poetry which he would work through to its full impact over the years of his collaboration with the Surrealists. It was a magazine with a minute circulation, and Artaud gave as his editorial address that of the cheap hotel near the place de Clichy where he was staying at the time. His contacts in the artistic and literary life of Paris began to grow as his output increased. He met several painters associated with the Surrealist group during this period – André Masson, Joan Miró and Jean Dubuffet.

The most exciting development in Artaud's life at this time was the beginning of his career in films. In the experimental first film of Claude Autant-Lara, *Fait Divers*, he played the role of a lover who is strangled to death in slow motion. After that, Louis Nalpas was sufficiently convinced by the exceptional facial beauty and distorted but expressive gestures that Artaud demonstrated on screen, and he began to use his influence to secure parts in the commercial cinema for his cousin. The first of these was in an energetic film entitled *Surcouf*, directed by Luitz-Morat on location in Brittany from July to September 1924. Artaud played a traitor who falls over the edge of a cliff in this spectacular adventure film, in a genre that was riotously successful in the pre-sound era French cinema. The response to Artaud's appearance was good, and he briefly believed that he could be a film star. And to some extent this would happen, with his appearances in two of the greatest films of the late 1920s, Abel Gance's *Napoleon* and Carl Theodor Dreyer's *The Passion of Joan of Arc*. But the cinema would also become a source of anguish and bitter failure for Artaud during his erratic engagement with it over the next ten years.

The event that initiated Artaud's literary career was his 1923–4 correspondence with Jacques Rivière, editor of *La Nouvelle Revue Française*. The prestige of the magazine attracted Artaud as a young poet, but his work was manifestly inappropriate for its conservative pages under Rivière's editorship. Its next editor, Jean Paulhan, was to be a great supporter of Artaud and to publish a great deal of his work. Rivière, however, approached Artaud's jagged poetry as a literary problem to be examined, discussed and solved. The correspondence concerns Artaud's view of the fragment – the 'failed' text – as more vital and exploratory than the 'whole' or 'successful' poem. In writing fragments, Artaud articulated his independence from and refusal of the coherent, unified aesthetic object. His fragments failed to incorporate themselves within a specific poetic culture; this intentional failure ensured that they would be banished into the territory of the self which was Artaud's only subject matter. While they exist within a tradition of fragmentation which includes much Romantic poetry, and the works of Baudelaire and Rimbaud, Artaud's fragments are exceptional in their willed upheaval and contraction of the language of poetry and the imagery of the self. Artaud's letters to Rivière form a correspondence about communication whose axis is silence, erosion and abandonment. The one poem which Artaud inserted in the published version of the correspondence is entitled *Cry*. In his letters, Artaud anatomizes the creative process of fragmentation. He deals with his incapacity to write a poem, and with the crystalline paralysis and pain of his mental apparatus as it tries to seize and formulate poetic imagery, failing abjectly to do so. What Artaud does grasp, in writing a lucid self-criticism which meshes with his poetry, is the substance of fragmentation. Confronting a poetic language that has been shattered by the exertion of writing at all, Artaud structures deep and disciplined insights into the emergence of the creative act.

In his initial letters to Rivière, Artaud declares his intention of transforming his 'shreds' into literary poems. He will write through feelings of loss, absence and desperation, in order to do this. Rivière gives Artaud blank encouragement in the project. He asserts that with due effort and concentration, Artaud will soon be able to produce poems that are 'perfectly coherent and harmonious', in the way that poems of *La Nouvelle Revue Française* had to be. Artaud attempts this and fails. He brings back that fragment of failure as the material to be submitted to Rivière, and asks for it to be sanctioned, given 'authenticity' and literary existence. Rivière has no direct answer to this, but he proposes that their correspondence on Artaud's poetry should be published instead of the poems themselves – the framework rather than the substance. He wants to present the correspondence as a unique document of poetic struggle: unique, and therefore universal, For this reason, he proposes to suppress his and Artaud's names. Artaud furiously refuses this. He wants his own intentions to be apparent: 'Why lie, why attempt to put on a literary level a thing which is the scream of life itself, why give an appearance of fiction to what is the ineradicable substance of the soul, which is the groan of life?'[7] For Artaud, the incoherent, inherently wild and vocal material of poetry must be exposed in all its independent and explicit pain, so that its fragmented sounds can be given breath and life. In that way it will express itself. Artaud's feeling of separation is the only thing which is whole, and not fragmented: 'I can say, truthfully, that I am not in the world, and that is not just an attitude of the mind.'[8]

Over twenty years later, in the August 1946 introduction to his *Collected Works*, Artaud recreated his relationship with Jacques Rivière (who died shortly after their correspondence closed), and with the 'sacrosanct' magazine which he edited. The absences and erosions which had formerly saturated Artaud's language had long since disappeared, and he now wrote fluently of his language as being dangerous and volatile. It is the inverse of the 'failed' language which had been at stake in the Rivière correspondence: 'If I drive in a violent word like a nail, I want it to suppurate in the sentence like a hundred-holed ecchymosis.'[9] He now attributes Rivière's premature death to a virulent contact with Artaud's language:

> . . . there is the corpse of a dead man. This man was called Jacques Rivière towards the beginning of a strange life: my own.
>
> So, Jacques Rivière refused my poems, but he did not refuse the letters by which I destroyed them. It has always seemed very strange to me that he died shortly after publishing these letters.
>
> What happened was that I went to see him one day and told him what there was at the heart of these letters, at the heart of the bonemarrow of Antonin Artaud.
>
> And I asked him if he had understood.
>
> I felt his heart rise up and split apart in the face of the problem and he told me he had not understood.
>
> And I will not be surprised that the black pocket which opened up in him that day diverted him away from life much more than his illness . . .[10]

The issue of *La Nouvelle Revue Française* containing Artaud's correspondence with Rivière appeared on 1 September 1924. Artaud's letters attracted great interest through their resolutely physical imagery of devastated cerebral processes of creation. For Breton, now directing the Surrealist movement as the leading avant-garde and anti-bourgeois group in Paris, the correspondence was vivid imagery from an insurgent unconscious mind, and he proposed a meeting with Artaud. On 7 September, Artaud's father died in Marseilles. At a lecture given during his stay in Mexico, twelve years later, Artaud spoke of that moment:

I lived to the age of twenty-seven with an obscure hatred of the Father, of my own father in particular, until the day when I saw him die. Then, that inhuman rigour, which I had often accused him of oppressing me with, fell away. Another being left that body. And for the first time in our lives, my father held out his arms to me. And I, always so restless in my body, I understand that all through life he had been made restless by his body, and that there is a lie to being alive, against which we are born to protest.[11]

The meeting with Breton and Artaud's subsequent induction into the Surrealist movement followed soon after the funeral of his father.

At first, Artaud had been resistant to Breton's invitation to join, and wrote to Dr Toulouse's wife: 'I am much too surrealist for that. And I always have been, and I know what surrealism is. It is the system of the world and of thought which I have always made for myself.'[12] But by early October 1924 he was a recognized participant of the Surrealist movement. It was a time of great activity for Artaud. During the same period, Abel Gance offered him the role of Marat in the film he was preparing to direct, *Napoleon*. In the course of October, Artaud was introduced to all the members of the Surrealist group; he formed strong friendships and creative collaborations with a number of the members, notably with André Masson and Robert Desnos. But the only enduring, life-long relationship was that between Artaud and Breton himself, despite the often brutal and patronizing insensitivity which Breton displayed towards Artaud. The two men were the same age. While Artaud had been working largely in self-absorption, using his own body and thought processes as the generating material for the explorations of his written work, Breton had been developing a gregarious, quarrelsome self-assurance in the literary life of Paris for over five years. He had already passed through the formative experience of automatic writing, *The Magnetic Fields*, with Philippe Soupault in 1919, and the subsequent violent divergence of his Surrealist group from the Dada participants associated with Tristan Tzara. At the two other points of great crisis and productivity in Artaud's life – 1937 with his journey to Ireland and 1946 with his return to Paris – it was towards Breton alone that Artaud would direct appeals for his incendiary projects to be approved or verified.

October 1924 was also the month in which Breton's first *Manifesto of Surrealism* was published, and in December, the first issue of the Surrealists' magazine *La Révolution surréaliste* appeared. For two years, until November 1926, Artaud involved himself with varying degrees of intimacy in the activities of the Surrealist group. He allied himself to their project of superseding bourgeois society by a revolutionary liberation of unconscious life, using dreams, trances and magical rituals to produce a fertile utopia of instinctual creativity. While Artaud was deeply interested in gestural rituals and mediumistic states of prophecy, he would never contribute individually or collectively to the Surrealists' automatic writing, where the text or image came as directly as possible from humorous collisions and paradoxical juxtapositions emerging from the unconscious mind. This was a writing and painting without super-vision, shot through with an undirectable spontaneity. As such, it was anathema to Artaud, who equated loss of intention in writing or painting with a catastrophic vulnerability. In the years of his theatre projects, this desire to control a flexible subject matter, even one in terminal disarray, extended to gesture with Artaud's advocation of the director's predominance over text and actor. In the context of Surrealism, Artaud believed that whatever debris or fragments he had managed to grate and grind from his unconscious should be his to manoeuvre to and beyond their limits.

Artaud rapidly changed the course of the Surrealist movement. His vehement and emotional presence disrupted the placid reliance of the Surrealists on their dreams to furnish the imagery for their poetry and painting. Artaud introduced new approaches and con-cerns into the movement. With his ferocious invective against social and religious leaders, and writings about drug addiction and physi-cal suffering, he threatened the group's complacent tendency to move towards imagery of ideal communities and loving, subser-vient women. In 1952 Breton would remember the 'impulsion' Artaud exerted on the movement to develop a language 'stripped of all that could have lent it an ornamental character' – a language that was intended to be 'scathing and glowing, but glowing in the way that a weapon glows'.[13] In much of Artaud's work, language is indeed presented as an arsenal of weapons and in terms of the violent upheavals it could precipitate, as an 'instrument to be forged' or a 'machine of instant utility'.

A mark of Artaud's initial influence on the group was his nomina-tion as Director of the Surrealist Research Centre on 23 January 1925, only three months after he had joined the group. Until then the Centre had been open for the public to come in and record their dreams; Artaud immediately closed it to the public. He wanted the

Surrealists to participate in disciplined research towards a 'devalu-
ation of all values', but they were an extraordinarily disorganized
and erratic group, capable of concerted action only under Breton's
direct orders. The activities of the Research Centre fell apart over
the following three months, and it closed altogether in April. This
contributed to the loss of Artaud's original euphoria about the
movement. But his publications in the second and third issues of *La
Révolution surréaliste* partly compensated for this. His article
defending the use of opium appeared in the second issue, published
on 16 February 1925. Artaud argues that the drug addict has an
inalienable right to destroy himself, and this right negates all social
control and legislation. The same issue included Artaud's text
rejecting suicide, since 'I have already been dead for a long time, I
am already suicided.'[14] He does, however, approve of the kind of
suicide which is planned and determined to the last detail. (One
Surrealist who performed just such a suicide was the erotic painter
Pierre Molinier. Having meticulously planned his suicide for
decades, he shot himself after becoming impotent. As a pre-
arranged signal to his friends of what he was about to do, Molinier
sent his cat to the local bar.) Artaud would return to the question of
suicide in 1947 with his book *Van Gogh the Suicide of society*.

The editorial control of the third issue of *La Révolution surréaliste*
was given over entirely to Artaud. He was determined to use this
opportunity in the same way that he had wanted the Surrealist
Research Centre to be used. The magazine would become the
orifice for assaults upon all the social, religious and medicinal
bodies which the Surrealists held in contempt. Artaud conceived of
a series of open letters that would accomplish this. They would
convey a powerful and intimate refusal to their addressees. Artaud's
idea for a written expectoration of direct insults cut across the
predilection of many of the Surrealists for a vague and inoffensive
esotericism. Breton in no way participated in the composition of the
letters. He would later claim that Artaud had led the Surrealist
movement in a dangerous direction with this material, which was
far more unsettling and precarious than the anguish experienced by
Breton and Soupault from too close an involvement with automatic
writing. Artaud's issue of *La Révolution surréaliste* was published on
15 April 1925. It was to be the only issue edited by Artaud; Breton
himself directed the fourth issue in July, which contained nothing
at all by Artaud.

Artaud gave the title *1925: End of the Christian Era* to his issue of

La Révolution surréaliste. He wrote a substantial part of the magazine's content himself, and all of it was instigated by him. There were five open letters – 'Address to the Pope', 'Address to the Dalai Lama' and 'Letter to the Schools of Buddha', all written by Artaud alone; 'Letter to the Rectors of European Universities', by Artaud in collaboration with Michel Leiris; and 'Letter to the Head Doctors of Asylums', by Robert Desnos at Artaud's suggestion. The Pope, the rectors and the doctors all endure the force of Artaud's demolishing wrath. He threatens the Pope: 'we are thinking of another war, war on you, Pope, dog.'[15] The letter to the doctors contains an adamant refusal of the social constitution of madness, which was to remain constant from this point onward in Artaud's work: 'All individual acts are anti-social. Madmen are the victims *par excellence* of social dictatorship.'[16] But in addressing the Dalai Lama and the Buddhists, Artaud displays a yearning for the destruction of the Western world and the creation of a new, liberated flesh. When Artaud came to rework these letter-manifestos for his *Collected Works* in 1946, his gauche adulation was abruptly overturned. The Eastern mystics are dismissed as 'filthy Europeans after all',[17] and subjected to an invective the intensity of which parallels that directed at the Pope. By 1946, Artaud's fury was all-consuming.

Artaud's association with the Surrealists gave him a notoriety which made the publication of his poetry easier to accomplish. Artaud wrote an abundant quantity of poetry during the early part of his Surrealist period. The sheer volume of this poetry seems to defy the voids and paralyses which were its subject matter. Artaud had developed his poetry's content since the time of his letters to Rivière. He believed that what he had to say was inexpressible, and that very inexpressibility – so immediate and so painful – should be the fertile substance of his poetry's investigations. Writing at the borderline between control and spontaneity (the nearest Artaud would come to the Surrealists' automatism), he directed his poetic language as fragmentary incursions into a territory of physical suffering and dispossession. For Artaud, the creative gesture was always doubled by its own loss and obliteration. In 1946, to introduce his work to a British readership, Artaud wrote a letter to Peter Watson, the art editor of the magazine *Horizon*. In this letter – never in fact published in *Horizon*, as intended – he put the poetry of his Surrealist period into perspective:

> I made my debut in literature by writing books to say that I could write nothing at all; when I had something to say or write, my thought was the thing most refused to me. I never had ideas, and two very short books, each of 70 pages, are concerned with this profound, deep-rooted, endemic absence of all ideas. These are *The Umbilicus of Limbo* and *The Nerve-Scales*.[18]

By 1946 Artaud had dispensed with the question of having ideas in his poetry. He was preoccupied with gestural violence and the body, and would write: 'Ideas are the voids of the body.'[19]

The Umbilicus of Limbo appeared in July 1925, three months after Artaud's issue of *La Révolution surréaliste*. Its original title had been *Opium Hanging, or The Shittiness of the Social Mind*, but this was changed for its publication by Éditions de la N.R.F. (the publishing wing of the magazine in which the Rivière letters had appeared), in a relatively large edition of 800 copies. The book had a portrait of Artaud by André Masson, and one of the texts was a poetic interpretation of a Masson painting. The principal material of the book is the poetry of fractures and abandonments which the Rivière letters had announced. Artaud's poetry ricochets between expositions of nervous pain and of linguistic incapacity:

> a sensation of acidic burning in the limbs,
> muscles twisted and as though cut to ribbons, the feeling of being glass and as though breakable, a fear, a retraction from movement, and noise. An unconscious disarray in walking, gestures, movements. A will perpetually tautened for the most simple gestures,
> renunciation of the simple gesture,
> an exhaustion which is staggering and central, a kind of exhaustion which breathes . . .[20]

The Umbilicus of Limbo is an amalgam of diverse materials, initiating a practice that extends throughout Artaud's work, including the theatre manifestos. The book also incorporates numerous fragments from letters, and the scenario *The Spurt of Blood*, where an illogical sequence of violent actions prefigures the concern with destiny and global catastrophe in Artaud's later theatre. He writes: 'The sky has gone mad.'[21]

The development of a poetry which could burst out into other creative structures was continued in Artaud's next collection of short texts, *The Nerve-Scales*, published only a week after *The Umbilicus of Limbo*. Artaud revised several of his letters to Génica Athanasiou into documents of exasperation and independence. The absences which Artaud felt to be proliferating within his poetry were intimated by the visual appearance of the book itself, with expanses of blank pages reinforcing the dense splinters of poetry. The writing also includes the manifesto 'All Writing is Pigshit', which carries an invective assault parallel to that of the open letters published in *La Révolution surréaliste*. Artaud denounces all literature, and announces a movement towards a furious silence that could still be utterly expressive. He was to explore and research that silence, with texts, screams and images, all through the rest of his work.

The Nerve-Scales was initially published in an edition of only seventy-five copies; again, Artaud's work was illustrated by Masson. The book was reissued in March 1927 in a larger edition, together with Artaud's most sustained poetic text from the Surrealist period, *Fragments of a Journal from Hell*. This text, with its Rimbaudian title and use of direct address, is among the most powerful of Artaud's writings. It persistently and brutally projects Artaud's paralysis and pain by concentrating on the anatomical: 'I am man by my hands and my feet, my guts, my meat heart, my stomach whose knots fasten me to the putrefaction of life.'[22] Horrific images of birth and death are intricately layered between Artaud's fragments, generating a final exclamatory break from the immediacy of physical collapse and anguish: 'I work in the unique duration.'[23] With *Fragments of a Journal from Hell*, Artaud had reached a point of exhaustion in his poetry, and he abandoned it. (A further volume was published by Robert Denoël in 1929, *Art and Death*, which collected several of the Surrealist poetic texts from 1924 to 1926, alongside diverse material. These texts bring death and sexuality into intimate proximity, and alternate between poetic evocation and analytical self-exposure.) Artaud's poetry was submerged by the explosion of his work into the fields of film and performance. The crisis of his expulsion from the Surrealist movement reinforced his feeling that his poetry was obsolescent. It was twenty years before poetry surged back as a means of expression for Artaud.

Artaud's break with the Surrealists accumulated over the year that followed the publication of his issue of *La Révolution surréaliste* and his two collections of poetry. The divergences between Artaud and the other participants of the group, particularly Breton, came about from a number of factors. The Surrealists despised Artaud for his dependence upon commercial film-acting to make his living.

During the period June 1925 to July 1926, Artaud appeared in three films – *Graziella*, directed by Marcel Vandal in Italy; *The Wandering Jew*, another film by Luitz-Morat; and Abel Gance's *Napoleon*, which had been delayed by financial problems. Artaud played Marat, one of the leaders of the French Revolution, in Gance's legendary silent film. Artaud's acting in this particular film possesses an extraordinary command of facial distortion. When Marat is murdered in his bath, this power is dispelled, and Artaud's face becomes a startlingly composed deathmask.

In addition to his film-acting, Artaud was planning to create a theatre company. It was to be directed by himself, Roger Vitrac – a poet who had already been expelled from the Surrealist movement in 1924 – and the writer Raymond Aron. This was to be the Alfred Jarry Theatre, named after the outrageous French philosopher and playwright who had written *Ubu Roi*. Artaud formulated a manifesto which, while not acknowledging any connection whatsoever with the Surrealists, nevertheless aimed the Surrealist concerns with dreams and magic at the performance space. A programme of forthcoming performances was drawn up. But the Surrealists were opposed to Artaud's plans, and generated friction between Artaud, Vitrac and Aron; this led to the collapse of the project, just before Artaud's exclusion from the Surrealist group. At that time, November 1926, Artaud wrote a further manifesto, *Manifesto for an Aborted Theatre*, emphasizing the need for a theatre where every gesture would 'carry behind it all the fatality of life and the mysterious meetings of dreams'.[24] But at this point Artaud was 'forever dissuaded' that such a theatre could ever be brought into existence. The acrimony with which Breton in particular attacked the project stemmed largely from the view that theatre was intrinsically bourgeois and profit-orientated. This was the time of the Surrealists' alliance with the French Communist Party.

The core of the quarrel between Artaud and Breton was about revolution. Breton intended to commit the Surrealist movement to political action. He believed that Surrealism had done all it could in the field of literary provocation, and that it should now turn to social action, while retaining autonomy within the structure of the Communist Party. Over the coming years, Breton was to realize that the two movements – artistic and political – could not be reconciled or integrated, and by 1935 he had broken with Communism and was reviling Stalin. But in 1926 he viewed Artaud's theatre project as counter-revolutionary, to the extent that Artaud had to be expelled from the Surrealist group. For Artaud himself, revolution could not be political; it had to be physical. This is one of the few positions he held consistently throughout his life. He dealt with it again in 1947 when Breton invited Artaud to participate in the International Surrealist Exhibition at a commercial art gallery. Artaud refused, pointing out the contradiction of Breton's position, and complaining: 'It is very probable that after this you will turn your back on me as happened between us in 1925, that you will spit on my carcass and my ideas, vomit on me from head to foot. . .'[25] Revolution, for Artaud in 1925-6, was vital to his concept of the physical experiments to which his new work would lead. By transforming the body – through gesture, film, theatre and writings – the world itself would concurrently be seismically reformulated: 'the revolutionary forces of any movement are those capable of unbalancing the fundamental state of things, of changing the angle of reality.'[26] All political structures and organizations were anathema to Artaud; similarly, he was repelled by the systematization which psychoanalysis could inflict upon his volatile temperament. He derided the Surrealists for setting up the idea of revolution as an untouchable fetish, and denounced Marxism as 'the last rotten fruit of the Western mentality'.[27] (He did, however, have a certain regard for the Royal Communism of the Incas.) This dispute over the meaning and application of revolution grew during the final year of Artaud's adherence to the Surrealist group; finally, it precipitated his expulsion.

The final reason for Breton's animosity towards Artaud was Breton's own anxiety about the direction his movement should take. Many of Artaud's contemporaries saw Breton's move towards Communism as a last-ditch attempt to keep Surrealism alive after the loss of its original euphoria and innovations, and viewed the proposed amalgamation of Surrealism and Communism as a hopelessly inept manoeuvre. By contrast, Artaud had injected a new and vital set of concerns into the group, with great commitment and passion, while Breton's leadership was undergoing a period of severe lassitude in the early part of 1925. It is conceivable, then, that Artaud's expulsion was a self-defensive move of desperation on Breton's part, to secure his leadership. But, by the end of 1926, Artaud was himself growing increasingly desperate. In addition to his tensions with the Surrealists, the extinguishment of his poetry, and the stalling of his theatre project, he was torn between Génica Athanasiou and Janine Kahn. He wrote to Janine Kahn on 13

November 1926: 'I am in a state of possession, of negation – of constant destruction . . . If I were only capable of being faithful to myself, if I could only formulate, translate by the raw working of my temperament what I feel, what I think of myself, I would be nothing but a long scream.'[28] He was contemplating suicide, or a total escape from his life in Paris: 'I want to have the strength to need nothing at all, to exist in a state of absolute disappearance.'[29]

The official exclusion of Artaud from the Surrealist group came with a meeting at the Prophet café. Artaud was to give the exact time as nine o'clock on the evening of 10 December 1926; Breton remembered the event as taking place around the end of November. (Breton's collaborator on *The Magnetic Fields*, Philippe Soupault, was excluded at the same time as Artaud; over the years, Breton would summarily expel all the group's original members, with the notable exception of Benjamin Péret.) Artaud refused to justify his projects against Breton's accusations. His acute independence, and his belief that the Alfred Jarry Theatre in no way compromised the integrity of his work, prevented this. He would later write: 'What separates me from the Surrealists is that they love life as much as I despise it.'[30] The quarrel between Artaud and the Surrealists ground on for several years. In response to an attack published by Breton, Péret, Louis Aragon and Paul Éluard, Artaud wrote two short pamphlets levelled against the Surrealists. (The edition of the second of these, *Full Stop*, was pulped by the printer since Artaud failed to pay for it.) In *Full Stop*, Artaud assesses the trajectory of his involvement with the Surrealists:

> Surrealism came to me at a time when life had succeeded perfectly in exhausting me, making me despair, and when there could no longer be any solution for me but madness or death. Surrealism was that potential hope, unseizable and probably as deceitful as any other, but which pushed me, in spite of myself, to attempt a last chance, to cling onto any kind of ghosts for the slight degree to which they might succeed in fooling my mind. Surrealism could not give me back a lost substance . . .[31]

Now, he would work in 'a solitude without compromise'.[32]

During the period from 1927 to 1930, Artaud applied the work he had been formulating in his time with the Surrealist group to film and theatre. The Alfred Jarry Theatre was reactivated early in 1927, despite Artaud's assertion two months earlier that he was 'forever dissuaded' that it could work out. This period of three years was one of great experimentation, but also of abject failure, for Artaud's projects. He was working in isolation on material that demanded effective collaborations. His film work, in particular, is one of the crucial areas of Artaud's creativity, but it has often been dismissed as an inconsequential footnote to the Surrealist cinema of Luis Buñuel, and to the enthusiasm of the Surrealist group at this time for the more delirious aspects of Hollywood cinema. Artaud envisaged a Surrealist cinema without the Surrealists. His film work exists in fragments, having been produced in difficult conditions and without the vehicle of a film under Artaud's direct control. As such, it can only be reconstructed through the interaction between Artaud's dispersed film scenarios and his flawed theoretical work upon the cinema.

Artaud is known as the writer of one of the three great examples of Surrealist cinema, *The Seashell and the Clergyman* (the other two being Buñuel's *Un Chien Andalou* and *L'Age d'Or*). But the film has the reputation of having been 'butchered' by its director, Germaine Dulac, who was insensitive to Artaud's intentions. Dulac was a prolific film-maker, associated with the Impressionist group which included Abel Gance. She had no connection with the Surrealist movement. It is certain that Dulac and her producers conspired to keep Artaud away from the shooting and the editing of the film – he had wanted to co-direct and act in it. They chose a time when they knew that Artaud would be contractually bound to his acting role in Carl Theodor Dreyer's *The Passion of Joan of Arc*. His original scenario of April 1927 came under a certain amount of revision before the shooting period of August to September 1927. The levels of alteration are evident from a consultation of the various stages of the shooting script. And the technical heaviness of the film, with its complex superimpositions and distortions, sits badly with the poetic clarity of Artaud's scenario, where information about the means to transfer the written image to the cinematic image is virtually non-existent. But it was his exclusion from the film-making process which particularly incensed Artaud, and led to the disruption of the film's première at the Ursulines cinema in Paris on 9 February 1928. Despite his exclusion from the Surrealist group over a year earlier, Artaud had considerable support from the Surrealists over the 'betrayal' of his scenario. It was Artaud's friend Robert Desnos who initiated the volley of invective directed at Germaine Dulac, and the showing ended in violence. Two accounts

– both of doubtful reliability – exist of Artaud's own participation in the brawl. In one, Artaud ran wild and shattered the cinema's mirrors, crying out: 'Goulou! Goulou!' In the other version, he was sitting quietly with his mother and uttered only one word during the uproar: 'Enough.'

After this event, *The Seashell and the Clergyman* was taken off the Ursulines programme, and it has resurfaced only erratically since then. The film was rejected by the British Board of Film Censors with the justification : 'The film is so cryptic as to be meaningless. If there is a meaning, it is doubtless objectionable.' The following year, 1928, the film was overshadowed by Buñuel's collaboration with Salvador Dali, *Un Chien Andalou*. Artaud claimed that this film, along with Jean Cocteau's *Blood of a Poet*, had taken displacement techniques and hallucinatory imagery from the film he had written (by 1932 he had partially reversed his attitude towards *The Seashell and the Clergymen*, claiming it to be a precursor of Buñuel and Cocteau's films). In fact, Germaine Dulac's interpretation follows Artaud's elliptical narrative of a priest's sexual obsessions with surprising fidelity; her visual pyrotechnics are all that obscure the essential substance of Artaud's scenario. But what was cinematically ungraspable by Dulac was Artaud's innovative project for the Surrealist cinema, which could not be carried through without a radical obliteration of cinematic history, and a reworking of the rapport between the film image and the film spectator.

In opposition to the dream-descriptions which make up the scenarios of the other Surrealists, such as Robert Desnos and Benjamin Péret, Artaud proposed not a translation of the dream and its content, but an exhaustive investigation of the systems of dreaming, to discover their mechanisms and their structures-in-collapse. In this way, he wanted to reconstitute the violence and independence of dreaming, as a process directly projected into cinematic imagery; his aim was to 'realize this idea of visual cinema where psychology itself is devoured by the acts'.[33] His theoretical objection to Germaine Dulac's film was that it returned his scenario to a flat depiction of the dream from which it had issued. Artaud had drawn his primary material for the scenario not from one of his own dreams but from the transcript of a dream written down by his friend Yvonne Allendy. This distance was necessary for Artaud to launch the analysis of the dreaming process, which is tangible at the intersection between his scenarios themselves and the writings

upon them. In juxtaposition, these two elements envisage a reinvention of cinema based around its visceral, transforming propul-
sion against the spectator's physical reflexes and reactions. It is
through its superficial scrupulousness and theoretical vacuity that
Dulac's film veers away from Artaud's filmic concepts.

The Seashell and the Clergyman was only part of Artaud's film
work, which runs at a tangent to the emerging Surrealist cinema of
Buñuel. He wrote or prepared fifteen scenarios altogether, including an adaptation of Robert Louis Stevenson's *The Master of Bal-
lantrae* and a commercial project entitled *Flights*. He also wrote an
autobiographical scenario about his relationship with Génica Athanasiou, *Eighteen Seconds*, which ends with the male character's
suicide. He tried to interest the German Expressionist cinema and
its offshoots in Hollywood in a scenario for a horror film about a
mass murderer, *The 32*. *The Seashell and the Clergyman* was the
third of these scenarios. The most extraordinary of Artaud's
scenarios is the final one, *The Butcher's Revolt*, which he intended to
direct himself and for which he drew up an intricate, though
mathematically inaccurate, budget. The scenario was written early
in 1930, during the era of upheaval between silent and sound
cinema. It concerns a 'madman' who is obsessed by meat and the
treachery of women. He is involved in a series of violent altercations
and headlong, senseless chases.

Previously, Artaud had expressed adamant opposition to the
introduction of sound. In a lecture given on 29 June 1929 at the
Surrealists' favourite cinema, the Studio 28 in Montmartre,[34] he
said:

> There is no possible identification between sound and image. The
> image presents itself only by one face, it's the translation, the trans-
> position of the real; sound, on the contrary, is unique and true, it
> bursts out into the room, and acts by consequence with much more
> intensity than the image, which becomes only a kind of illusion of
> sound.[35]

Sound, then, would have to be excised from the image, in order for
the image to develop its autonomous evocatory force. In his
scenario *The Butcher's Revolt*, Artaud attempted to come to terms
with what he saw as the destructive interrelation of sound and
image. Certain isolated, obsessive phrases (such as 'I've had enough
of cutting up meat without eating it') were allowed into the
scenario, typographically emphasized and enclosed in boxes. They

served to give density to the visual imagery, which would thereby rebound from the image/sound collision with greater power. In a note accompanying the publication of this scenario in *La Nouvelle Revue Française* of June 1930, Artaud summarized the content of his imagery: 'eroticism, cruelty, the taste for blood, the search for violence, obsession with the horrible, dissolution of moral values, social hypocrisy, lies, false witness, sadism, perversity'. All this would be visible with 'the maximum readability'.[36]

This approach to film sound parallels that used by Artaud eighteen years later with his recording for radio *To have done with the judgement of god*, where the sound effects – screams and beatings of percussion instruments – appear in tension with Artaud's poetry of expulsion and refusal. The violent physical gesture cuts across the escalating rush of poetic imagery. In *The Butcher's Revolt*, the primacy of the image broke with the 'filmed theatre' which predominated in the cinema of the time (and which Artaud detested), while stressing the spatial quality of the reinforced sounds which would be employed: 'The voices are *in space*, like objects.' These spoken interjections would be made between interruptions of the image, against a void black frame. Since, for Artaud, representation works on a temporal level – sound and image repeat themselves to convey themselves – his determination to introduce a spatial rather than temporal element into film sound signals a denial of the pull towards diminution which he believed any completed, represented aesthetic object makes. In Artaud's project for the Surrealist cinema, the film has its axis in the human body, which must be immediately present, shattered and dense. In parallel terms, the Italian Futurist film manifesto of November 1916 (which Artaud must have been aware of) had demanded 'polyexpressiveness' and proposed 'filmed unreal reconstructions of the human body'. Later, in the arena of interaction between the film and its performance space, the early Lettrist cinema developed ideas similar to those of Artaud. At the first screening of Maurice Lemaître's *Has the film already started?* in 1951, buckets of water and insults were thrown at the audience by the film-maker. With a scenario that amalgamated volatile, confrontational elements into a spatially flexible and eruptive structure, Artaud proposed a cinema which would be acutely resistant to representation.

Artaud failed to find the money to finance *The Butcher's Revolt*. His theoretical work on the cinema tailed off, while he continued to act in films. Dreyer's *The Passion of Joan of Arc*, like Gance's

Napoleon, provided Artaud with a rare opportunity to demonstrate his individual acting style – the expressive gestural control of his performance oscillates between paroxysmal seizure and emotional grandeur. He plays the monk Massieu who accompanies Joan of Arc to the stake, and had a tonsure for the role. He desperately wanted to play the part of Frederick Usher in Jean Epstein's film of Poe's *The Fall of the House of Usher*, but was turned down with a certain derision. He also earned his living in this period with films of variable quality, including Léon Poirier's *Verdun, Memories of History* (1927), Marcel L'Herbier's *Money* (1928), and Raymond Bernard's *Tarakanova* (1929), in which Artaud appears as a gypsy lover. He made the first two of his journeys to Berlin to act in Franco-German co-productions, and had a role in G. W. Pabst's film of Bertolt Brecht's *The Threepenny Opera* (1930). It was a film which Artaud despised for its 'vulgarity and its complete disorientation'.[37] In fact, most of these films constituted painful, humiliating work for Artaud, especially Raymond Bernard's patriotic blockbuster *The Wooden Crosses* (1931), in which Artaud plays an enthusiastic soldier who tries to leap out of his trench towards the Germans, crying: 'I shit on you, swine!' At the end of the film, he is shot dead. This 'abominable work' led to the exhaustion of Artaud's engagement with cinema of any kind, and he would conclude: 'I am ever more convinced that the cinema is and will remain the art of the past. You cannot work in it without feeling ashamed.'[38]

An innovative theory of cinema emerges from the fragments which Artaud wrote at the time of *The Seashell and the Clergyman* and *The Butcher's Revolt*. This theoretical film writing, like all Artaud's work, exists in a state of flux, with points of abandonment followed by periods of resurgence. His proposals for a Surrealist cinema are contradictory and often incoherent, and are best seized at the intersection between film and some other creative apparatus, notably in his letters about the cinema. The letter was always a privileged site of articulation for Artaud, in which polemical exhortation could be allied to direct address. He writes with the greatest intensity of visualization about his lost, unrealized projects. The narratives of Artaud's scenarios are constructed from a deeply individual and heterogeneous material, designed to probe wide and complex matters such as the origins and systems of dreaming. The amplitude and potential of Artaud's concept of cinema must be sought in the spare traces left by his letters, his theoretical writings, his scenarios, and the sections of Dulac's *The Seashell and the*

Clergyman which remain attached to Artaud's imagery.

Artaud perceives filmic representation as an abyss. From the time of the Rivière correspondence, he had evoked a two-way trap in which his activities fell apart. He was faced on one side by the disintegration of his language through inarticulation – the slippage which the image suffered as it was brought into the textual form. On the other side, he was trapped by the loss of the 'completed' text into representation – its original and unique bond with Artaud was stolen at the moment the text became available to an audience. His hostility towards representation endured, achieving its most forceful expression in *To have done with the judgement of god*, by which time the concept of representation was inextricably and maliciously social for Artaud. He believed that the cinema relies on deceptions of light, sound and movement, and on institutions; as such, it intrinsically denies his idea of the filmic work in direct and hostile contact with the body. But Artaud recognized that the element of mediation is an intractible given in the cinema, and had to be both ambushed and worked with. His film work attempted to confront and tear the image from representation, to move it into proximity with the spectator's alert sensorium.

The force of Artaud's film language emerges from its density. Elements are suppressed or subtracted in order to be articulated. Narrative is broken, while the image is pounded down to compact visual sensation. Artaud wrote: 'search for a film with purely visual sensations in which the force would come from a collision exacted on the eyes'.[36] (There is a striking parallel here with the eye-slitting – enacted on the screen and in the moment of viewing it – at the beginning of Buñuel's *Un Chien Andalou*, which was in preparation at the time of *The Seashell and the Clergyman*'s première.) For Artaud, then, the concentrated impact which his film might possess results from the isolation of jarring elements within the textual system, producing a dynamic and spatial inscription of images. With a project such as *The Butcher's Revolt*, the imagery's visceral charge would be accentuated by the breakdown of filmic space, into which isolated voices could be juxtaposed.

Artaud's concept of cinema veers away from film fiction, with integrated sound and image, towards a kind of documentary interaction of chance and control. All his scenarios project an atmosphere of darkness, blood and shock on the border between these two points. An endless doubling is present there; divisions are shattered between reality and fiction, between danger and entertainment. Artaud's film writings inhabit borderlines, charting the trajectory of what he called 'the simple impact of objects, forms, repulsions, attractions'.[40] His crossing of textual borders implies a negative push: the image stays in the domain of the image, or else risks annihilation. In their collapsing of borders, Artaud's film texts move towards a fall into catastrophe, towards what cannot be realized. In Artaud's film, the image aimed for and the spectator aimed at would be in a state of magnetic, negative interaction. The film image would be at its most stripped-away and expressive, at its most resistant to the process of representation. The film spectator would be the exposed subject of what Artaud called 'the convulsions and jumps of a reality which seems to destroy itself with an irony in which you can hear the extremities of the mind screaming'.[41]

For Artaud, the cinema was literally a stimulant or narcotic, acting directly and materially on the brain. He called his project 'raw cinema'.[42] While probing unconscious processes and dreaming, it would also demand a more immediately physical contact between the cinematic image and the spectator. Like Artaud's Theatre of Cruelty of the early 1930s, this language of film could only work once. It could give birth to only one, unique film. And it would avoid the spoken word as something constructed only in order to repeat itself, using instead an imagery compacted together from chance, control and the body.

Artaud's project for the Surrealist cinema is irreparably lost. It cannot stand on the strength of its celluloid imagery alone, unlike Buñuel's cinema, which has acquired a powerful enigma due to the relative critical silence of its maker. Artaud's cinema oscillates between imagery and commentary, like his drawings of the 1940s. The meshing of sound and image which Artaud feared in 1929 also terminated the first rush of Buñuel's cinema. Since then, only hybrid amalgamations of documentary and narrative cinema (such as Georges Franju's *The Blood of the Beasts* of 1949) have in any way approached the collision of blood and chance which Artaud envisaged for the cinema. He wanted a film which could face and seize fragmentation. His spectator would be placed at the edge of the capacity to evaluate, while being subjected to a swarm of impulsive and expulsive forces which would necessitate a transformation of the viewing position, and instigate resistance to the process of representation. Artaud's own position within the history of Surrealist cinema is one that parallels that interrogative resistance.

The Alfred Jarry Theatre existed at the same time as Artaud's film projects, from 1927 to 1930. While the film work was disciplined within its mainly textual confines, the Alfred Jarry Theatre generated a disorganized sequence of provocative public performances. It applied a confrontational Surrealism to the performance space with a wild and humorous impact. In this way it contrasts with Breton's Surrealism of the period, which was becoming increasingly sedentary. Rather than receiving a renewed creative input from its unsteady alliance with the French Communist Party, the Surrealist movement was embedding itself firmly in insular literary concerns. Apart from Breton's occasional forays into heckling at theatres, the initial strategy of experimental performance – which had characterized the time of the Dada-Surrealism collaboration – was now long forgotten. The Alfred Jarry Theatre took over that crucial aspect of the Surrealists' work, though Artaud would deny any rapport with Breton's Surrealism. He wanted this non-theatrical theatre, directed by writers and poets, to pre-date and negate the Surrealist movement; the evocation of the name of Jarry (whose work had been at its most outrageous in 1896, the year of Artaud's birth, with the première of *Ubu Roi*) assisted in this. The Alfred Jarry Theatre had no system or argument behind it whatsoever, unlike Artaud's subsequent Theatre of Cruelty. In this respect alone, it was close to Dada. On a basic level the theatre would serve as a public space where the writers Artaud, Vitrac and Aron could demonstrate their work.

The texts written by Artaud around the Alfred Jarry Theatre emphasize his unscrupulous attitude towards the theatre. Even during his deepest involvements with theatre, Artaud would say that he hated it as he loved it. The Alfred Jarry Theatre was not 'an end but a means'.[43] It was driven by an utter disrespect for the unity and sanctity of the play or theatrical text which was to be presented: 'The Alfred Jarry Theatre has been created to help itself to the theatre, and not to serve the theatre.'[44] Artaud dismissed the idea that theatrical spectacle should work as an illusion. The performances would be actions, revealing the 'pure brutality' of their concerns – physical compulsion and 'vibration', dreams and hallucinations. Artaud wrote of 'Hallucination chosen as the principal dramatic medium'.[45] This concern with the unscreened action extended to the staging of the performances. No sets would cushion the hysterical sensory overload of the planned performances. Artaud expected to exert an extreme and visceral captivation upon his audience. The subject matter would be a 'synthesis of all desires and all tortures',[46] and its performance would sustain this with the exclamatory surge of sound that is also evoked by the film writings. Even during the performance intervals, loudspeakers would be used to intensify the atmosphere, 'to the point of obsession'.[47]

With such an extraordinary set of intentions, the Alfred Jarry Theatre was to suffer a painful career. It was a theatre without money – Artaud was virtually destitute throughout this period. It was also a theatre without rehearsals – though this generated a certain eruptive spontaneity in the predetermined actions, which was attractive to Artaud. His collaboration with Vitrac and Aron became increasingly stormy as the project managed to sustain itself over a period of years. The first performances, on 1 and 2 June 1927, demonstrated the friction of disparate individuals who had formed a tenuous theatrical alliance. Although Artaud would write of the need to produce a 'manifesto-play, written in collaboration'[48] between the three participants, no such homogeneous arrangement was possible. Three separate works were performed, Artaud's contribution being a textless sketch entitled *Burnt Belly, or the Mad Mother*. The second programme came seven months later, on 14 January 1928, with a programme that combined theatre and film. A film by the Russian director Vsevolod Pudovkin, *The Mother*, was screened in protest against its censorship in France; then, the final act of a play by Paul Claudel – whom the Surrealists despised – was performed against the author's wishes, as a gesture of derision. The Surrealists had come to the event to disrupt it, but changed their minds when Artaud declared from the stage that Claudel was 'an infamous traitor'. A temporary reconciliation ensued between Breton and Artaud, for the period which included the première of *The Seashell and the Clergyman*. The animosity between Claudel and Artaud was to persist, with Claudel dismissing Artaud's work in 1947 as 'the imaginings of a madman'. The Surrealists broke with Artaud again at the third set of Alfred Jarry Theatre performances, of the Swedish writer August Strindberg's *Dream Play*, on 2 and 9 June 1928. The performances, which Artaud both directed and acted in, had been funded in part by Swedish nobles. Breton objected to this, although in the past he had accepted patronage from the Swedish aristocracy at the Surrealists' exhibitions. The Surrealists disrupted the performances. At first Artaud sided with the Surrealists to dispel the provocation, claiming that he had staged the play only to protest against the Swedish government's oppressive treatment of Strindberg, and against society in general. But at the second performance Aron called the police, and several Surrealists were arrested, including Breton. A complete play by Vitrac – *Victor, or The Children in Power* – was staged as the fourth project of the Alfred Jarry Theatre. The play, directed by Artaud on 24 and 29 December 1928 and 5 January 1929 (Artaud could only hire theatres at times when nobody else wanted them), was the last work of the Alfred Jarry Theatre. Although Artaud was offered patronage by the Viscount de Noailles, who funded films by Man Ray, Buñuel and Cocteau, the Alfred Jarry Theatre ended in recriminations between its participants.

Both Artaud's film writing and his Alfred Jarry Theatre have a movement towards breakdown and silence, which culminates in 1930. Through 1929, Artaud and Vitrac continued to work in circumstances of great friction at resuscitating the Alfred Jarry Theatre. To advertise their no-longer existent theatre, they executed a sequence of photo-montages at the beginning of 1930, with images of their bodies being decapitated, multiplied, and in violent conflict. The accompanying, ineffectual brochure, *The Alfred Jarry Theatre and the Public Hostility*, had to be written by Vitrac since Artaud's condition was deteriorating into one of acute nervous depression. No longer able to afford the hotel room he had been occupying in the rue de la Bruyère, Artaud had gone to live with his mother, who had moved from Marseilles to Paris after the death of her husband, to be nearer her children. Struggling with his constant addiction to opium, and with the failure of his work, Artaud began to contemplate different civilizations and apocalyptic imagery. He had met the young publisher Robert Denoël, who commissioned from Artaud a free adaptation of an English gothic novel, Matthew Gregory Lewis's *The Monk* (1794). Artaud, who could read no English, made use of a literal transcription of the novel into French. He expanded passages to accentuate the work's opposition to social and moral constraints, left entire chapters intact, and cut long digressive or poetic sections altogether. He was to some extent ashamed at having to work as a kind of translator, but he also tried to develop *The Monk* for the cinema. He had several dark and atmospheric photographs taken to illustrate his preferred scenes from the novel, in order to try to interest film producers. As with all such efforts on Artaud's part, this project failed. But it is notable that in June 1930 he sent a set of the photographs to the founder of the Italian Futurist movement, F. T.

Marinetti, who was now an official poet of Mussolini's Fascist regime and an influential figure in the Italian cinema. In his creative and financial desperation, Artaud was envisaging a move to Italy to undertake his projects.

The two years leading up to the summer of 1931 were intensely difficult for Artaud. He was now nearly thirty-five years old, and his attempts to produce films and theatre had utterly disintegrated. Since he had also abandoned poetry in 1926, his creative silence was now almost total. He was in a state of extreme poverty, moving back and forward at frequent intervals between his mother's flat, film-location hotels, and cheap hotel rooms around the place de Clichy. A brief affair with an actress from the Alfred Jarry Theatre, Josette Lusson, ended bitterly. His drug addiction, his nervous pain, and his sense of isolation from artistic groups such as the Surrealist movement, all compounded this breakdown into silence. The terrible lassitude of this period might well have proved terminal, but it was finally broken for Artaud on 1 August 1931, when he witnessed the event that precipitated his project for the Theatre of Cruelty: the performance of Balinese dance theatre at the Colonial Exhibition in Paris.

2

The Theatre of Cruelty

When Artaud saw the performance of Balinese dance theatre in August 1931, it released a great influx of imagery and formulations about theatre and the body into his writings. Very soon, he began to call this new stage of his work 'The Theatre of Cruelty'. The images jarred against and contradicted each other for a period of four years. At the final point, in May 1935, when Artaud sought to realize these images on the stage of a Parisian theatre, they fell apart again. When they resurfaced, it was as the motivation for a series of exhausting and testing journeys which led Artaud to his asylum incarceration. At times during the four years when Artaud was preoccupied with a theatre of compulsive gesture and physical crisis, his work came together with a rare precision and discipline, resulting in the manifestos and texts which became the collection *The Theatre and its Double*. But for most of this period Artaud suffered from the creative incapacities, and the personal indignities and refusals, which had destabilized and blocked the earlier stages of his work. His attempts to stage a spectacle that would demonstrate and crystallize his dreams about the theatre met with relentless failure, paralleling that of the drug detoxifications he endured in these years.

The Theatre of Cruelty was born out of a long period of Artaud talking to himself about theatre, then swinging that monologue around as a series of violently polemical manifestos addressed to an indistinct audience of literary figures and financiers. Only one man supported Artaud consistently through this period of grinding self-interrogation as a means of transforming culture – Jean Paulhan, who had succeeded Jacques Rivière as the editor of *La Nouvelle Revue Française*. In the face of much opposition from the other writers working on the magazine, Paulhan gave Artaud a degree of encouragement and patronage which was otherwise almost entirely absent. During this time, Artaud lived in a miserable poverty that relented only for short periods, when he had money from one of his film-acting parts or was on the ephemeral upswing of one of the projects to stage his theatre.

During its thirty years of notoriety, the Theatre of Cruelty has often been called an impossible theatre – vital for the purity of inspiration which it generated, but hopelessly vague and meta-phorical in its concrete detail. One of the most influential practi-tioners of Artaud's work in the 1960s theatre, the Polish director Jerzy Grotowski, believed that to use Artaud's theatrical proposals superficially would be to debase and negate them, and to carry them through with absolute fidelity would lead to a catastrophic state of collapse, where actions could no longer have any meaning. Artaud's demands for the Theatre of Cruelty envisage the director's extremely rigorous imposition of his vision on the actors and the audience: a creative but volatile chaos would result. For Artaud, the Theatre of Cruelty is a precise action in which the final impact swallows all the means. It is a dangerous theatre, which threatens the identities and bodies of both participants and spectators. It aims for immediacy, and cannot be staged twice; consequently this theatre distrusts words, since the textual is necessarily repetitive. But these proposals, which originated in intentions which fiercely resisted all compromise, slipped away from their source. Artaud, who promised that his theatre of gestures and cries would embody magic and supernatural forces, saw his work reduced to a low-budget, social event staged, in exasperation, on the boards of a boulevard theatre.

Artaud attended one of the performances of the dancers from Bali, in the Indonesian Islands, at the massive Colonial Exhibition in the Vincennes Forest, south-east of Paris. He had been on film-location for the early part of the summer, acting in *The Wooden Crosses*, and returned to Paris in mid-July. Soon after witnessing the performance on 1 August, he began writing through his respon-ses as an article for *La Nouvelle Revue Française*. Part of his reaction was conveyed in a long letter sent to Jean Paulhan while Artaud was on a trip to Anjou. His experience of the Balinese theatre and its gestural intensity was the first of the three events of 1931 which provided the essential groundwork for the Theatre of Cruelty. The same year, Artaud 'discovered' a painting in the Louvre museum by Lucas van den Leyden, which inspired his concept of the spatial and aural dimensions of his theatre; and he saw two films by the Marx Brothers, *Animal Crackers* and *Monkey Business*, which gave to the Theatre of Cruelty its attachment to laughter as a force of wild destruction and liberation.

For Artaud, the Balinese theatre contained all the elements

which he had included in the Alfred Jarry Theatre as a strategy of resistance to the predominantly textual and psychological European theatre. It had the centrality of the gesture, and the subordination of the textual; it had discipline and magic. What Artaud added from his own temperament was the ferocity and the attack upon society with which his idea of the theatrical gesture would be charged. Above all, in 1931 Artaud was envisaging a truly dangerous theatre which would threaten the security both of the word and of the world with its unique performances. From the Balinese dance theatre he formulated a project for an entirely new language of physically articulated signs – his actors would become compact, evocative hieroglyphs. Artaud's spectacle would be so immediately articulate that it could largely dispense with any textual element. He was bluntly rejecting an entire theatrical tradition: 'A European conception of the theatre requires the theatre to be mixed up with the text, that everything should be centred around the dialogue, which is considered as the point of departure and arrival.'[1] Artaud perceived no text in the Balinese theatre. He was attracted by fragmentary, violent gestures which were suddenly cut and abandoned, producing an 'autonomous and pure creation, under the angles of hallucination and of fear'.[2]

Already, Artaud was introducing the theme of the double into his theatre. This ambiguous element grew to saturate Artaud's theatrical writings. The double would become both life itself, as it emerged from his theatre, and also the malicious force which could steal Artaud's work out from under him. The final element of inspiration Artaud drew from the Balinese theatre was the predominance of the director, as opposed to the playwright: 'It is a theatre which eliminates the author to the profit of what we, in our Western theatrical jargon, call the director; but he becomes a kind of magical organizer, a master of sacred ceremonies.'[3] Artaud's perception of the Balinese dance theatre was certainly exaggerated, and was expanded in scope to help build upon his fledgling proposals. Jerzy Grotowski has said that Artaud's vision of Balinese dance was 'one big mis-reading',[4] and that he mistakenly gave supernatural resonances to gestures that dealt only with the concrete and the everyday. But Grotowski misses the point. Artaud's commitment was to creating a new theatre, not to interpreting an ancient one.

The second inspirational event which contributed to the Theatre of Cruelty came in September 1931, when Artaud saw the fifteenth-century Leyden painting *The Daughters of Lot* at the Louvre. Its multiple perspectives of calamity and sexuality had a profound effect upon him. Artaud perceived parallels between this painting and the Balinese dance theatre he had seen in the previous month. He took many of his friends to see the painting during the coming years, while the Theatre of Cruelty was developing, and he gauged their responses as though they were witnessing a theatrical spectacle. Artaud drew upon the distorted spatial architecture of the painting and its concerns with incest and apocalypse to pinpoint the form and material he wanted for his new theatre. He began to consider the painting as the result of a finely elaborated creative direction, like that governing a theatrical spectacle which could be 'composed directly on the stage, realized on the stage,'[5] without dialogue or text. Artaud perceived the painting as also assembling and conveying explosions of sound to punctuate its visual impact. He wrote a text which communicated these impressions within the framework of a provocative and exasperated rhetoric about the theatre's relationship to society: 'I say that the present state of society is iniquitous and is ready to be destroyed. If it is the work of theatre to preoccupy itself with this, it is even more so that of the machine-gun.'[6] He entitled his text 'Direction and Metaphysics'; his individual use of the term 'metaphysics' related to an active poetry which his theatre could wield as though it were a weapon. But the term was initially seen as vague and anachronistic when Artaud read part of his text at a conference on 'The Destiny of the Theatre' in Paris on 8 December 1931. Artaud's contribution was received in a 'deathly silence'.[7] Just two days later, Artaud read a fuller, revised version of his text at the Sorbonne, to an appreciative response. Jean Paulhan took it for publication in *La Nouvelle Revue Française*, and Artaud's tentative theatrical images and proposals began to expand into fully-fledged manifestos.

The first two components in the Theatre of Cruelty were dance and painting; the third was film. Artaud included his reponse to the Marx Brothers' film *Monkey Business* in the text 'Direction and Metaphysics'. The film had been released in Paris in mid-October 1931, and Artaud wrote a review of that film and *Animal Crackers* (which had opened in December 1930) for *La Nouvelle Revue Française*. The films were stripped apart for what they could contribute to Artaud's theatrical project. By this period, Artaud's disillusionment with his own film work was total. As a result, all his reactions to the Marx Brothers were channelled from the medium of film to the medium of theatre. Although the Theatre of Cruelty was to be majestically austere and grave, Artaud saw a value in counterpointing the seriousness of his work with 'the sense of true humour and of the power of physical and anarchic dissociation in laughter'.[8] He accorded the Marx Brothers' films an almost unique distinction by calling them surrealistic, and praised their sense of 'complete liberation' and their 'tearing of all reality'.[9] From the Marx Brothers' films, Artaud developed his insistence on the necessary danger of the chance, disruptive event in his theatre. This event would have the potential to break destructively through the meticulous preparations of the performance, to precipitate tragic and poetic collapses of the action. Artaud viewed with awe the power of laughter to induce abrupt transformation. He stressed the quality of revolt in the outbursts of noise and movement in the Marx Brothers' films. His response to these films added a vital, insurgent element to his emerging theatrical concerns: 'And the triumph of all that is in the kind of exultation – at once visual and sonorous – that these events catch in the shadows, in the degree of vibration which they attain, and in the kind of powerful anxiety which their accumulation ends by projecting into the mind.'[10]

While these crucial events in Artaud's imaginative life were following closely upon one another during a period of four months at the end of 1931, his personal life was one of great solitude and misery. At this point of creative fertility in Artaud's work, his financial situation was at its most critical. He was still contemplating leaving Paris altogether, as he had done the previous year with his plan to make experimental films in Italy; now he wanted to leave for Berlin to work as a theatre director. But he was unenthusiastic about the productions, such as those of Piscator and Meyerhold, which he had seen in Berlin during his film-acting stay there in 1930: 'I believe in the real action of the theatre, but on the scale of life. After that, I don't need to say that I consider to be useless all the attempts made recently in Germany, in Russia and in America, to make the theatre *serve* immediate social and revolutionary goals.'[11] As always with Artaud's work, society was to be refused, not served; and revolution was to be the result of a process of grinding and violent reconstruction in the theatre, emerging from an overwhelming transformation of physical space and time, rather than from the actions of a didactic or socially useful theatre.

The French theatre, too, seemed closed to Artaud. He began to consider a play by Büchner, *Woyzeck*, in terms of a production he could stage to introduce his new ideas. He tried to persuade the

directors Louis Jouvet and Charles Dullin to allow him to stage the
play in their theatres, without success, and he was also contemplating a further collaboration with Vitrac. Artaud's ideas for the
theatre met with interest from a small group of people, among them
Jean Paulhan; his practical plans for theatrical spectacles, however,
elicited almost no response at all, and this situation would continue
for almost four years. In order to survive and not to have to take on
too many humiliating film roles, Artaud tried to think of other
sources of income. In September, he was planning to give lessons in
dramatic and cinematic art to beginners, in the conference room at
the offices of his publisher, Robert Denoël. He appealed to Paulhan
to find him pupils, but the plan foundered. The following month he
had to apply for an emergency grant from a governmental writers'
fund, and was awarded three thousand francs. He had been moving
from hotel to hotel in the Pigalle district during the autumn
months, struggling to exist when the money from his film role in
The Wooden Crosses ran out; but during October, he moved in with
his mother again at her flat in the fifteenth *arrondissement* of Paris.

During 1932, Artaud's gradual construction of the Theatre of
Cruelty developed, while his material difficulties gave the theatrical
writings an impassioned edge of desperation and imminent disintegration. January 1932 was the month when Jean Cocteau's first
film, *Blood of a Poet*, was released. Artaud attended a special
screening for writers on 19 January, and the success of the film
made him intensely jealous. He believed that *Blood of a Poet* had
stolen imagery from *The Seashell and the Clergyman*, and that it was
one of the 'little babies'[12] (along with Buñuel's films) that had
emerged from the film he had written and was now reclaiming.
Artaud demanded that Paulhan give him a regular column in *La
Nouvelle Revue Française* where he could pour out his bitterness
against the cinema, but this was denied him. The Cocteau première
was valuable for Artaud, since there he met the great homosexual
novelist André Gide. Despite Gide's distaste for the theatre, he
would support Artaud's theatrical projects sympathetically over the
next few years. It was also at this time that the final death throes of
the Alfred Jarry Theatre occurred, long after it had last staged a
spectacle. Vitrac had been threatening to appropriate the theatre's
name for his own ends. Artaud sought to prevent this by suggesting
a joint performance, to be staged at a derelict cinema in Montmartre, with the ostensible aim of resuscitating the Alfred Jarry
Theatre; the event failed to materialize.

Artaud's financial position eased slightly. He wrote three imaginary travel articles for the popular illustrated magazine *Voilà*, setting his richly evocative and detailed writings in Shanghai, Tibet and the Galapagos Islands. He had been to none of these places. He secured a position as an assistant director to Louis Jouvet on the production of a play entitled *The Village Confectioner*. This mundane work gave Artaud the opportunity to harass Jouvet with his own plans for the theatre, and to suggest nightmarish, exaggerated imagery for the production. In a letter to Jouvet, Artaud wrote:

> What would you say, for the dream at the end, to twenty mannequins, five metres high, of which six would represent the most characteristic people in the play, with their outstanding features, appearing suddenly, and waddling along with a solemn air to the rhythm of a warrior march which would be chosen to be strange, packed with Oriental consonants, in burstings of Bengal lights and rockets. Each of these people could have an attribute, and one of them could, for example, carry the Arc de Triomphe on his shoulders.[13]

Artaud was deeply upset that all his suggestions to Jouvet were ignored. He had hoped to convince Jouvet that they should collaborate on the productions that would realize Artaud's theatrical concepts, but Jouvet had no intention of being taken down such a dangerous road. Artaud had another plan to make a little money, this time by teaching acting classes for beginners, and he intended to use Jouvet's rehearsal room when it was empty. During this period he also helped Denoël's American publishing partner, Bernard Steele, to translate a novel by Ludwig Lewisohn, *The Case of Mr Crump*, into French as *Crime Passionnel*. Unlike *The Monk* this translation was undertaken solely for financial reasons, and Artaud felt humiliated by the work.

In March 1932, Artaud formed the idea that his theatre should receive the backing of *La Nouvelle Revue Française*. It would then be sure to attract serious attention. To this end, he set to work persuading Paulhan to allow him to call his project 'The Theatre of the N.R.F.'. He also began to collect the support of weighty literary figures such as Gide and Paul Valéry for his theatre, so that he could use their names to generate funding for the spectacles he wanted to stage. He also wrote a new text to highlight the magical aspects of his theatre and its capacity to create transformations.

This text, *Alchemical Theatre*, was initially intended for *La Nouvelle Revue Française*; instead, it was translated into Spanish and published in the Argentinian magazine *Sur*. It would not appear in French until Artaud's collection of theatre essays was published in 1938. The entire conception of Artaud's theatre at this time was determined by the fact that he was writing his texts and manifestos for established literary periodicals. His ideas were vividly phrased and packed with imagery. To some extent, this contributed to their impact – Artaud's writings on the theatre developed a highly attractive and open style which helped to articulate difficult and challenging ideas. But, in the context of the literary periodical, he was never able to spell out in explicit detail the wild dreamings and physical upheavals of his planned theatre. This created an obstacle to his ambitions, since his readers could not imagine how Artaud would transpose his literary formulations into living, cruel gestures in the performance space. In the spring of 1932, a short-lived theatre strike took place in Paris; this gave Artaud the opportunity to declare his desire for the present theatre to be destroyed, so that his own theatre could be born:

> In the course of the month which has just ended, the theatres, cinemas, dancehalls and brothels of Paris attempted the first gestures of a strike, moreover purely demonstrative, which allows us to see what the true theatre would gain from the disappearance of all that which currently does the job of pouring out spectacles, and which, theatre, music hall, cabaret or brothel, must all be sewn into the same sack.[14]

In April, Artaud had to interrupt the momentum of his theatre projects in order to make another trip to Berlin. This time he appeared in a crime thriller, *Gunshot at Dawn*, directed by Serge Poligny at the famous UFA studios. Artaud had one of the leading roles in the film, playing a murderer nicknamed 'The Trembler' because he made his hands shake to distract the suspicions of the police. Artaud considered it shameful work. But he had some regard for the professionalism of the German Expressionist cinema, with which he came into contact during his stays in Berlin. He appreciated its sophisticated lighting techniques, and was impressed by its ability to produce commercially successful films from stylistic experiments and challenging subject matter. Berlin, at that time, had a highly charged atmosphere. Its economic situation was precarious, and the ascendancy of Adolf Hitler's Nazi party was evident. Artaud's temperament during his stay fluctuated between acute depression about his material circumstances and the tortuous pace of his theatre's development, and a nervous exaltation about the spectacles he was confident that he would soon direct. The accumulating collapse of a previously affluent and secure society in Berlin was fascinating to him: 'The streets are full of admirably dressed beggars, some of whom must be the former middle-classes.'[15] He believed that society in Berlin was preserving itself from catastrophe only by a thin screen of decadence, fashion and gluttony. In the years to come, especially at Rodez, Artaud would recall seeing and even speaking to Hitler in May 1932 at the Romanisches Café in Berlin. This was just plausible. (The Roman- isches Café was a fashionable literary and political meeting-place – like the Dôme in Paris – of the kind that Hitler had once fre- quented.) In May 1946, shortly before his release from Rodez, Artaud was to evoke a dialogue he had had with Hitler in this café. According to Artaud, Hitler had told him that he was going to impose Hitlerism on Europe just as gratuitously as he might have imposed Hip-Hip-Hoorayism; Artaud retorted to Hitler that he was crazy to lead people by ideas rather than by actions, and a violent brawl ensued.

When Artaud returned to Paris at the end of May, he began to push hard for the success of his planned 'Theatre of the N.R.F.'. But he was moving too fast for the Parisian literary milieu. On 26 June he gave a magazine interview in which he confidently declared that *La Nouvelle Revue Française* had already agreed to fund the theatre, and that he was going to direct it. He also claimed the support of famous writers who had not yet given authorization for their names to be used, and he asserted that the details of where his theatre was going to be based would be fixed in only a few days' time. In fact, *La Nouvelle Revue Française* had tentatively con- sented only to the exploitation of its name; no funding had been agreed. The owner of the magazine, Gaston Gallimard, was furious with Artaud. It was a terrible setback: Artaud had to write a retraction, and he tried to placate Gallimard through the inter- mediary of Paulhan by claiming that his responses in the interview had been fabricated. He managed partially to salvage the situation – his writings promoting the new theatre could still be published in the magazine, but now he would have to find a new title for it.

During July and August 1932, Artaud worked on a manifesto to launch his new theatre. He supported himself through this frenetic

period by taking a small part in another film directed by Abel
Gance, *Mater Dolorosa*, and he was still living with his mother. He
spent the summer months agonizing over his manifesto, which he
drafted repeatedly and was never completely happy with. He also
had a problem in deciding on the theatre's title. Artaud was initially
thinking of 'The Alchemical Theatre' or 'The Metaphysical
Theatre', but he rejected these since they would be 'a huge laugh
for people who weren't well-informed'.[16] He also considered 'The
Theatre of the Ordeal', 'The Theatre of Evolution', and 'The
Theatre of the Absolute' (Paulhan's suggestion). Finally, he settled
on 'The Theatre of Cruelty' (*Théâtre de la cruauté*). When Artaud
communicated this title to the press, a number of magazines mis-
read his handwriting. It was announced that Antonin Artaud had
founded a new theatre entitled 'The Theatre of the Crust' (*Théâtre
de la croûte*).

For Artaud, 'cruelty' could embody in one word all his creative
preoccupations and his personal suffering. He resisted the superficial resonances of blood and murder attached to the word,
believing that the idea of cruelty could communicate a remaking of
worlds. It produced many images. In theatrical terms, it conveyed
the exhaustive testing which was to be the work of the director: 'It
means to go to the very end of all that the director can exert on the
sensibility of the actor and the spectator.'[17] For Artaud, cruelty also
generated outward from the theatrical space to encompass all conscious and intentional action. In effect, it formed an elaborated
version of the intentional and hostile Surrealism which Artaud had
promoted in 1925. He was to include several of the multiple definitions of cruelty from 1932 in his collection of theatre essays, *The
Theatre and its Double*. They were mainly drawn from letters to
Paulhan. Cruelty 'means rigour, application and implacable
decision, irreversible and absolute determination.'[18] Just as the
current Parisian theatre would have to be destroyed for Artaud's
Theatre of Cruelty to emerge, so the term 'cruelty' encapsulated the
tight rapport between life and death:

> Above all, cruelty is lucid, it is a kind of rigid direction, submis-
> sion to necessity. No cruelty without consciousness, without a kind
> of applied consciousness. It is consciousness which gives to the
> exercise of every action in life its colour of blood, its cruel touch,
> since it must be understood that to live is always through the death
> of someone else.[19]

On 20 August Artaud completed his manifesto for the Theatre of Cruelty. He sent it first to Gide, who was thinking about translating an Elizabethan tragedy, *Arden of Faversham* (which had once been attributed to Shakespeare), for Artaud to use. Artaud put pressure on Gide to allow him to include his name and that of the play in the list of productions he was drawing up to reinforce his manifesto. But Gide was adamant that his name should not appear. He was worried about making commitments that he might not be able to fulfil. Artaud kept pressing, and Gide finally became angry; the manifesto appeared with only the title of the play. In the months that followed, Gide did translate *Arden of Faversham*. Artaud found the play tame, and it failed to meet his requirements. He complained to Paulhan that when the text of the play was stripped down to its essentials, as it had to be in his theatre, there would be little left for him to work with.

The manifesto was to be published in the October 1932 issue of *La Nouvelle Revue Française*; Artaud spent September undertaking the last revisions. He considered this written account of his plans to be flawed and inadequate. During the same period, he began to meet financiers who might fund his productions. In Paris, numerous businessmen and aristocrats were attracted by the prestige of investing in a new artistic spectacle. Artaud published a short article in the theatre magazine *Comoedia* to introduce his manifesto and to stress his opposition to the textual theatre:

> As to the works, we will not stage any written play. The spectacles will be created directly on the stage, with all the means that the stage offers, but with those means taken as a language with the same status as the dialogue of written theatre, or words. This does not mean that the spectacles will not be rigorously composed and *fixed* once and for all before they are played.[20]

The spontaneity of Artaud's theatre would emerge from his own role as its director; once the performance had begun, a cruel discipline would operate.

Artaud's manifesto constitutes the most livid attack, and the most challenging reformulation, that the modern theatre has ever endured. Elements from all three of Artaud's principal theoretical preoccupations of the previous year – Balinese dance, the Leyden painting and the Marx Brothers' films – were included in the manifesto. Artaud was envisaging a precise gestural and visual vocabulary for his theatre:

It is here that will intervene – in addition to the auditory language of sounds – the visual language of objects, of movements, of attitudes, of gestures, but on condition that they prolong their sense, their physiognomy, their assemblages to the point where they become signs, and make of the signs a kind of alphabet. Having become aware of this language in space – language of sounds, of cries, of lights, of onomatopoeia – the theatre owes it to itself to organize this language, by making people and objects become true hieroglyphs, and by helping itself to their symbolism and their correspondences to all media and on all levels.[21]

He also emphasized the necessity of 'LAUGHTER – DESTRUC-TION'.[22] And he saw the role of the theatre director as crucial in amalgamating volatile movements and images into disciplined spatial arrangements:

This kind of language of the theatre will constitute itself around the direction, which will be considered not simply as the refraction of the text upon the stage, but as the point of departure for all theatrical creation. And it will be in the use and manipulation of this language that the ancient duality between the author and director will fuse together, and be replaced by a kind of unique Creator, to whom will fall the double responsibility of the spectacle and the action.[23]

Artaud's spectacle would articulate physical crises and attitudes through cries and rhythmic movements. It would aim to nullify the textual. As with Artaud's film scenario of 1930, *The Butcher's Revolt*, spoken language would remain in the form of an intensified and incisive element, to be inserted without warning: 'It is not a case of abolishing the articulated word, but of giving words something of the importance which they have in dreams.'[24] Artaud's innovations were aimed at every aspect of the theatre space, the actor's work and the spectator. He wanted to create new musical instruments to reinforce the aural dimension of his spectacle. These instruments would produce strange vibrations and extremely loud noise. The lighting would be like 'arrows of fire'.[25] The entire spatial volume of the performance space would be explored; the barrier between the stage and the spectator would be obliterated, in order to facilitate a 'direct communication'[26] between the spectator and the spectacle. The spectator's viewing position would be reversed; the action would take place around the edges of the building, and the spectators would be placed in the centre, on revolving chairs. A central space was to be reserved only for the most important points of convergence in the spectacle's action. The building (rather than a theatre) in which the performance was to take place would be bare, undecorated. The actors, in spectacularly exaggerated costumes, would have to carry all the spectator's attention. For Artaud, the actor would function as the skilled instrument of the director's intention, able to articulate intricate physical states. At the same time, Artaud was willing to allow the introduction of an unstable element of chance, whereby the actor's power of gestural metamorphosis could transform him back from an instrument to an individual. In all, Artaud's concepts amounted to an attack on the spectator as well as on the stability of the theatre as an institution. His audience was still an unknown quantity. The Theatre of Cruelty would necessarily generate its own audience: 'First, this theatre must exist.'[27]

The response to Artaud's manifesto on its publication was hostile. Many people were disturbed by the extent to which Artaud had developed ideas that were antithetical and inassimilable to European culture. Embedded in his manifesto was a threat to language. If language was to be dissolved from words with definite meaning, into a substance of multiple gestures and cries that had a more direct, more visceral capacity for expression, then that threw into question all the weight that social, political and religious forms of expression carried. Artaud's concepts had implications which extended far beyond the arena of the theatre. Considerable opposition to Artaud grew from within *La Nouvelle Revue Française*. One of its leading critical writers, Benjamin Crémieux – who had supported Artaud's Alfred Jarry Theatre – now threatened to resign from the magazine if another word written by Artaud was published there. These repercussions continued until the end of the year, with Artaud leaning on his friendship with Paulhan and trying to maintain his connection with *La Nouvelle Revue Française* as the principal outlet for his theatrical writings. He was pleased by the extreme reaction to his plans, and indifferent to the fact that it was largely dismissive. He now believed that he would secure the capital necessary to finance a demonstration of his ideas. But his material circumstances were still difficult; in October, he took a small role in his third film of the year, *My Sister's Child*, directed by Henri Wulschleger.

In November, Artaud received an invitation to collaborate on one of the strangest projects of his life. The invitation came from the

Franco-American composer Edgar Varèse, whose music was in some ways a sonic parallel to Artaud's theatre, with its sudden percussive movements and fragmentations, and its explorations of space. Varèse was planning a musical event incorporating dance, light and great gestural movement, to be staged in the street. It was to be titled *The Astronomer*, and would deal with a huge and destructive star which both exhilarates and threatens the world's population. Varèse had already approached Robert Desnos in 1928, and now he wanted Artaud to attempt the libretto. Artaud had never heard Varèse's music, but the project fascinated him and he agreed to undertake it. He set to work and produced four movements of the libretto. Although he considered Varèse's proposal for a street performance, Artaud's libretto was set in a more enclosed space. He was envisaging a layered spatial arrangement of light and colour to counterpoint Varèse's music: 'No colour will be pure. Each shade will be complex and varied to the point of anguish.'[28] Varèse's music would finally overwhelm this space: 'The music will give the impression of a faraway cataclysm which envelops the room, falling from a breathtaking height.' In his libretto, Artaud evoked a physically grotesque and terrified population, like the characters of his final film scenario, *The Butcher's Revolt*: 'Display of horrors. The heads become more and more gross and menacing, stricken with stigmata, character-ized by symbols, in thick synthetic strokes, all vices and sicknesses.'[29] Their continual shouts were to be driven to a level of hallucinatory exaggeration by the sudden addition of other elements: 'All these texts are to be cut with passages of screams, of noises, of sonorous tornadoes which drown everything.'[30] This idea of the spoken word in collision with the scream would be explored again, much later in Artaud's work, with his 1947–8 radio recording *To have done with the judgement of god*. Artaud entitled his libretto for Varèse *There is no more Sky*. But he abandoned it at the end of the fourth movement with a fusion of 'violent percussions'. Varèse had returned to his base in New York, and wrote to Artaud a number of times during the course of 1933, urging him to complete the libretto and send it to him. Finally, in the early part of 1934, Artaud sent Varèse a typescript of part of the work he had done. By that time, Varèse was in a state of suicidal depression, which was to last for thirteen unproductive years.

Artaud's increasingly perilous nervous state and his consumption of opium were threatening to incapacitate him and destroy his

theatre plans. During 1932, he underwent an acupuncture treatment with some beneficial results. But at the beginning of December, he had to be hospitalized in the Henri-Rousselle clinic at the
Sainte-Anne asylum in Paris, for a detoxification cure. The treatment was expected to last for forty days. Artaud stayed there only
one night before the brutal cure, in an open ward of geriatrics,
became intolerable to him. He abandoned the treatment, against
medical advice, and was obliged to complete a questionnaire about
his opium addiction before leaving the clinic. He wrote of how
opium dissolved his anguish like sugar in water, and described the
painful process of detoxification:

> The sufferings are above all physical, intense cold, bitings in the
> muscles, sheets of pressure on the face and the nape of the neck,
> terrible seizure in the loins, all consciousness reduced at the moment
> of paroxysm to the state of a block of screaming pain, this sensation
> being so sharp and so strong that the entire consciousness identifies
> itself with it. On the other hand, a screen which was on the world
> seems to disappear, I find life again.[31]

He also described dreams he had experienced as a result of opium
use. Mythic figures would approach him in his room, become
human and 'slowly assassinate me, with patience and application'.[32]
In time, during his journey to Ireland in 1937 and through to the
end of his life, the visions became stronger, and Artaud would
bitterly accuse these waking hallucinations of being real – the
tangible demonstrations of social malice and sexual assault. He had
to fight constantly to maintain the integrity of his body. On his
release from the Henri-Rousselle clinic, Artaud transferred to a
private clinic and stayed there in isolation from 10 to 26 December.
The results were partially successful, and he was able to keep his
addiction under some degree of control through much of 1933 and
his great activity during that year. But the detoxification process
had left him deeply shaken. It had been an 'atrocious cure'.[33] He
returned to his mother's apartment, distressed and terribly poor.

With the new year, 1933, Artaud set to work to realize his plans
for the Theatre of Cruelty. It was to be a year in which he tried to
convey the desperate urgency of his proposals to a largely apathetic
audience. Artaud was well aware that the Theatre of Cruelty had to
be launched as a business venture as well as a revolutionary dream
about theatrical and physical transformation. In the first days of
January he rapidly produced a second manifesto for the Theatre of

Cruelty. His standing with *La Nouvelle Revue Française* was still delicate, and so Artaud designed this manifesto in the form of a brochure aimed at attracting financial interest. Robert Denoël and Bernard Steele published the brochure, and it included a subscription form for people to buy shares in the Theatre of Cruelty. Artaud added no vital innovations to his previous manifesto, but he expressed his project with a fluent concision and a sense of vision: 'The overlapping of images and movements will, by the conspiracies of objects, of silences, of cries and of rhythms, arrive at the creation of a true physical language based on signs and not words.'[34] He also introduced the first production to be staged by the Theatre of Cruelty. It would be a vast evocation of collapsed civilization entitled *The Conquest of Mexico*, for which he completed the scenario by the middle of January. The scenario dealt with the Spanish conquest of the Aztecs in 1519; it contained no fixed dialogue. Artaud's opposition to psychological theatre was evident in the declarations which accompanied his scenario: '*The Conquest of Mexico* will stage events presented in their multiple and most revelatory aspects, and not men.'[35] His project was sensationally ambitious in conception. Historical breakdowns and violent contradictions were to be exposed in all their magnificence and intricacy by Artaud's spectacle: 'In this collision of moral disorder and catholic anarchy with the pagan order, it will be able to make extraordinary conflagrations of forces and images spurt out, sown here and there with brutal dialogues. And this will happen through the struggle of man to man, carrying the most opposed ideas with them like stigmata.'[36] Artaud believed that when such huge-scale concerns and upheavals were drawn out on the stage, his scenario with its sixteenth-century setting would become absolutely contemporary.

At the beginning of 1933 Artaud formed an attachment to Juliette Beckers, the wife of one of Denoël's colleagues. On one occasion, Artaud went to see Juliette Beckers unexpectedly. He was in a state of nervous collapse, and she put him on her sofa and took off his shoes. His socks were full of holes, and Artaud began to sob at the humiliation of his position. He relied on his affair with Juliette Beckers for the support and sympathy which were so lacking in his life, begging her to give him moments of her time and confiding his bitterness at having to appeal for funding to stage his spectacles: 'A malicious fatality oppresses me. Like Lazarus, I have to nourish myself with the crumbs which fall from the table of the fortunate rich.'[37] His physical state was unstable during this period, and he had eye troubles which often made him fear going out into the street. One night in February, on the boulevard du Mont-parnasse, he found a sixteen-year-old girl named Anie Besnard sitting on a bench and weeping. She had run away from her family in Luxemburg, and was starving. Despite his own poverty-stricken condition, Artaud fed, helped and comforted the girl, and they became close friends. The border between paternal purity and incestuous jealousy in Artaud's attitude towards Anie Besnard was highly charged. Always resistant towards his own family, Artaud filled this absence with parallel relationships. He was dependent for approval on older men such as Paulhan and Gide (and Breton, who was the same age as Artaud), and had complex emotional relations with younger people such as Anie Besnard and Roger Blin. At the Rodez asylum, Artaud was to create his family of 'daughters of the heart' and would include Anie Besnard in it. In his letters from Rodez he made great demands on Anie Besnard which she could not fulfil. As a result, he began to believe that she had been murdered while travelling to see him at Rodez, and replaced with a spurious, unfaithful double who remained in Paris and married. But Artaud remained deeply fond of her, meeting her again often in the final part of his life when he was back in Paris, and writing to her: 'Each time I see you is the most beautiful day of my life.'[38]

While his affair with Juliette Beckers was declining, in March 1933, Artaud met another woman, Anaïs Nin, who would become a great source both of inspiration and of disillusionment for him. In 1933, Anaïs Nin – now renowned for her journals, essays and erotica – was living to the west of Paris in the village of Louve-ciennes with her husband, Ian Hugo. It was the period of her affair with Henry Miller, and she had already published her first book, on D. H. Lawrence. Artaud had known the psychiatrist René Allendy and his wife Yvonne for a number of years; he had discussed his film projects with them. (He had considered undergoing analysis with Allendy, but decided it would be useless; Allendy, who was known for his attachment to flagellation, considered Artaud to be a dangerous, homosexual drug addict.) It was through Allendy that Artaud met Anaïs Nin, at a dinner party at her home. Anaïs Nin was fascinated by Artaud, and he soon fell in love with her. In her journal she wrote of the impression Artaud had made upon her, and of his current reputation:

Artaud is the surrealist whom the surrealists disavowed, the lean ghostly figure who haunts the cafés but is never seen at the counter, drinking and sitting among people, laughing. He is the drugged, contracted being who walks always alone, who is seeking to produce plays which are like scenes of torture.

His eyes are blue with languor, black with pain. He is all nerves.[39]

Over much of the first half of 1933 Artaud worked on a project commissioned by Denoël, a biography of the third-century Roman Emperor, Heliogabalus. Artaud's research for the book entailed his spending many days in the Bibliothèque Nationale in Paris, reading books on Roman history, astrology and esoteric religions. It was at this point that he became actively interested in mysticism, magic and primitive mythologies. These concerns were fed into his work until the time of his asylum incarceration, four years later, and they also shaped the choice of destinations for Artaud's journeys of 1936 and 1937. By 1946, when he was released from the asylums, Artaud's views had altered significantly, and he viewed Catholicism and all Eastern religions as part of one huge and malicious apparatus (he had also grown to despise the Balinese by that time). Roger Blin reports that 'When Artaud came back from Rodez, he thought all that was the same business, that Rome and Tibet were the same shit.'[40] The book on Heliogabalus, which Artaud subtitled *The Crowned Anarchist*, was intended to make him some much-needed money. Denoël issued the book in a much larger edition than any of Artaud's previous books – around five thousand copies – although it proved to sell badly. To give his book a greater rhythmic force and fluency, Artaud dictated the final version of *Heliogabalus*. He displayed some hostility towards historical accuracy and authenticity: 'I have written this *Life of Heliogabalus* as I would have spoken it and as I speak it. I have also written it to help those who read it to un-learn history a little; but, all the same, to find its thread.'[41]

Heliogabalus was Emperor from the age of fourteen to eighteen. His reign was characterized by murder, incest, debauchery and an anarchic ridicule for the powers of government. Artaud structured his account of Heliogabalus's life around the breaking of borders and the expulsion of fluids, notably blood and sperm: 'Around the corpse of Heliogabalus – dead without a tomb, and cut apart by his police in the latrines of his own palace – there is an intense circulation of blood and excrement, while around his cradle, there is an

intense circulation of sperm.'[42] Artaud saw contradictions in the life
of Heliogabalus which accorded that life a great poetry of subver-
sion and physical extremity. He emphasized the imminent danger
of assassination throughout Heliogabalus's short reign, and paralleled it with his own permanent sense of coming catastrophe. He
inserted himself into his own narrative of sexual excess: 'I do not
judge what happened as History might judge it; this anarchy, this
debauchery pleases me.'[43] The atmosphere of the Theatre of
Cruelty, as Artaud's principal preoccupation during the writing of
Heliogabalus, permeates the book. Theatre in Heliogabalus's time
takes place in life, not on the stage; Heliogabalus's mother demands
cruelty first of all for herself, just as Artaud did; Heliogabalus
obstinately pursues the introduction of myths into life. The poetry
of Heliogabalus's life is also that of Artaud's theatre:

> There is, in all poetry, an essential contradiction. Poetry is the
> grinding of a multiplicity which throws out flames. And poetry,
> which brings back order, first of all resuscitates disorder, disorder
> with inflamed appearances; it makes appearances collide and brings
> them back to a unique point: fire, gesture, blood, scream.[44]

Finally, Artaud's book is swamped by its excremental vocabulary as
it narrates the Emperor's death: Heliogabalus is bloodily hacked to
pieces in a sewer, still in a provocative state of 'open rebellion'[45] at
the moment of death.

To Paulhan, Artaud revealed the degree of his affinity with
Heliogabalus, emphasizing 'the central figure where I have described myself'.[46] Anaïs Nin was close to Artaud during the period
when he was writing the book, and she described Artaud's wild
temperament after he had voraciously absorbed the prophetic
power of Heliogabalus's life:

> Artaud sat in the Coupole pouring out poetry, talking of magic, 'I
> am Heliogabalus, the mad Roman emperor,' because he becomes
> everything he writes about. In the taxi he pushed back his hair from
> a ravaged face. The beauty of the summer day did not touch him. He
> stood up in the taxi and, stretching out his arms, he pointed to the
> crowded streets: 'The revolution will come soon. All this will be
> destroyed. The world must be destroyed . . .'[47]

During the early spring of 1933 Artaud was also working on a
new theatre essay. He collected all his wide-ranging formulations
about cruelty in this text, and gave them a focus in the action of

plague. For Artaud, plague was something which could not be isolated or seized, but the power of transformation it could exert on bodies was devastating and inspiring. Artaud's determination to realize his theatre in the performance space was now in an advanced state of tension. The restless expansion of his creative ambitions extended to the texture of his writing in 'The Theatre and the Plague'. Plague was conceived not as a metaphor for Artaud's theatre, but as a kind of instrument of vision around which his multiple ideas for the Theatre of Cruelty could collect. Artaud's theatre needed an imagery which could convey both the raw viscerality and the potentially magical forces which he sought to give to his spectacles. Plague provided this imagery. 'The Theatre and the Plague' contained no details, systems or proposals. It passed from an evocation of the effects of plague to a desperate polemical exhortation. The parallel between plague and theatre as forces of creative upheaval was drawn out meticulously: 'The plague takes images which are asleep, a hidden disorder, and suddenly pushes them towards the most extreme gestures; and theatre too takes gestures and pushes them to their final point: like plague, it remakes the chain between what is and what is not, between the hidden potential of the possible and that which exists in materialized nature.'[48] Artaud emphasized the violent physical momentum and sense of release which his theatrical direction would instil in the actor. The disciplined actions which resulted would be more authentic and substantial than those in life itself. Artaud made use of the imagery of plague in claiming a kind of terminal and unassailable purity for the theatre he was dreaming about: 'The theatre, like the plague, is a crisis which is resolved by death or by healing. And the plague is a superior evil because it is a complete crisis after which nothing remains but death or an extreme purification.'[49] He closed the essay with a declaration of the extent of his commitment to this theatre, a commitment which was itself poised between death – by suicide – and creative action.

Still lacking the financial means to stage a spectacle which would transfer and realize this imagery in the theatre space, Artaud took it upon himself to perform the theatre essay itself. His reading of 'The Theatre and the Plague' took place at the Sorbonne on 6 April 1933, as part of a series of intellectual lectures organized by René Allendy. Anaïs Nin was present, and gave an account in her journal of Artaud's performance and his audience's reaction:

His face was contorted with anguish, one could see the perspiration dampening his hair. His eyes dilated, his muscles became cramped, his fingers struggled to retain their flexibility. He made one feel the parched and burning throat, the pains, the fever, the fire in the guts. He was in agony. He was screaming. He was delirious . . .

At first people gasped. And then they began to laugh. Everyone was laughing! They hissed. Then one by one, they began to leave, noisily, talking, protesting. They banged the door as they left . . . More protestations. More jeering. But Artaud went on, until the last gasp. And stayed on the floor . . .

He was hurt, wounded, baffled by the jeering. He spat out his anger. 'They always want to hear *about*; they want an objective conference on "The Theatre and the Plague", and I want to give them the experience itself, the plague itself, so they will be terrified, and awaken. I want to awaken them. They do not realize *they are dead*. Their death is total, like deafness, blindness. This is agony I portrayed. Mine, yes, and everyone who is alive.[50]

Two days later, Artaud had formed a more detached appreciation of his performance; he believed it had been a success, through its volatile and intentional oscillation between failure, grandeur, and 'the most complete clownishness'.[51] This lecture was the first of a number of confrontational events culminating in the Vieux-Colombier performance of January 1947, in which Artaud explored extremes of self-exposure, and worked at the border between an exhaustive attack upon society and an abandonment of all languages. He reworked his essay on plague over the next three years; when he formulated the plan to collect his writings on theatre into a book, 'The Theatre and the Plague' was immediately placed at the beginning, so as to provide a ferocious storm of imagery which would penetrate through to the subsequent texts with their more detailed proposals.

Artaud's relationship with Anaïs Nin was not sexual, despite his desire for it to be so. Anaïs Nin wrote: 'To be kissed by Artaud was to be drawn towards death, towards insanity.'[52] She told him that she loved only the poet in him, not the flesh and bones: '"Brother, brother," I said. "I have such a deep love for you, but do not touch me. I am not to be touched. You are the poet, you walk inside my dreams, I love the pain and the flame in you, but do not touch me."'[53] Artaud contented himself with this for some time; he was elated by Anaïs Nin's interest in the writing of *Heliogabalus*, and her silent attentiveness when he took her to see the Leyden painting around which he had constructed his essay 'Direction and Metaphysics'. He wrote to her: 'Several things draw us together *terribly*, but one especially: *our silence* . . . On the platform of the railway station, when I said to you: we are like two souls lost in the infinite spaces, I felt this fluid silence talking to me and it would have been capable of making me sob with joy.'[54] Artaud was frightened that his drug addiction would alienate Anaïs Nin from him, as had happened with Génica Athanasiou. They met often, either at Anaïs Nin's house in Louveciennes or at the Coupole café in Montparnasse. As the summer went on, Artaud grew increasingly dubious about the literary life led by Anaïs Nin, and unsettled by her intimacy with her father and with Allendy. He began to feel that she was manipulating him, as just one more writer in her circle. His feelings became dangerously intense: 'Artaud said, "What a divine joy it would be to crucify a being like you, who are so evanescent, so elusive." . . . I was frightened by his fervour when he said, "Between us, there could be a murder." '[55] In June Anaïs Nin went to stay with her father in the south of France, and on her return Artaud ended their relationship in bitterness and anger. Eight years later, while Artaud was interned at the asylum of Ville-Évrard, Anaïs Nin published a short story about him in English, *'Je suis le plus malade des surréalistes'*. The events of their relationship are described in the first part of the story, often taken directly from her journals or from Artaud's letters. Artaud is given the name 'Pierre', and is a poet who wants to start a Theatre of Cruelty. The second part of the story is set in a mental hospital, where the 'Pierre' character is now in a strait-jacket. Anaïs Nin, who did not visit Artaud at Ville-Évrard, gives her character speeches which she had drawn from a textbook on schizophrenia, and which she believed were close to Artaud's own declarations.

Between May and August 1933 Artaud wrote a short manifesto entitled *The Theatre and Cruelty*, which was intended to form another brochure designed to attract funds for his theatre. Artaud was now thinking specifically of staging *Woyzeck* at the Raspail 216 cinema, and he appealed to the American heiress Natalie Clifford Barney to help him find the capital to realize his project. But the plan collapsed, and the brochure was never printed; Artaud's manifesto remained unpublished until it appeared in *The Theatre and its Double* in 1938. His theatrical concepts were now developing towards a 'total spectacle' that would incorporate all the other arts:

'In practical terms, I want to resuscitate an idea of total spectacle, where the theatre will know how to take back from the cinema, the music hall, the circus and from life itself, all that which has always belonged to it.'[56] His sense of an oncoming violent catastrophe was articulated at the end of the text with keen anticipation:

> It is now a case of knowing if, in Paris, before the cataclysms which announce themselves, I will be able to find enough means of realization – financial and otherwise – to permit such a theatre to live; and this theatre will hold out in any case, because it is the future. Or we will see if a little real blood will be necessary, immediately, for this cruelty to be demonstrated.[57]

On 10 September Artaud left Paris by train for the south of France, to attempt a self-imposed detoxification in isolation. He stayed in the artistic centre of Saint-Paul-de-Vence, close to the Mediterranean, and travelled to Cannes and Nice. His publisher Robert Denoël sent him money, and he was able to live well at an expensive hotel. The detoxification was not a success. Soon after Artaud returned to Paris at the end of September, he found a room at the Villa Seurat, an artists and writers' community in Montparnasse (Henry Miller was to move there in the following year). He was supporting himself during this period with small radio parts, and in November to December he acted in a film by Fritz Lang, *Liliom*; he had appeared in a theatrical production of the same work in 1923. Although Artaud disliked the film, it was the last notable part he was given. Still possessing a remarkable facial beauty, he played the role of a guardian angel with wry detachment. It was also in 1933 that Artaud had his final, caustic words to say on the cinema. In an article entitled 'The Premature Senility of the Cinema', he attacked the way in which the sound cinema had irreparably broken away from his own inventive proposals, written at the end of the 1920s. Cinema was now lost, its magical and poetic potential squandered: 'The cinematic world is a dead world, illusory and cut up.'[58]

At the end of 1933, Artaud wrote the last of his essays on the theatre from this period. The remaining writings which make up his collection *The Theatre and its Double* – notably those dealing with the actor's respiration and gestures – were added in 1935, after Artaud had formulated his book project and after his production of *The Cenci*. The essay, 'No More Masterpieces', is an assault upon what Artaud perceived as the paralysis of language that resulted

from its having been written down and given a literary value and
status:

> Let's recognize that what has been said does not need to be said
> again; that an expression is worth nothing the second time, and does
> not live twice; that every spoken word is dead, and is crucial only at
> the moment in which it is spoken, that when a form is used it will no
> longer be useful and will suggest only that we should search for
> another form, and that the theatre is the only place in the world
> where a gesture, once made, does not start up again.[59]

Artaud was proposing a theatre that would be in a state of constant
self-destruction and self-reconstruction. It would gain its vitality by
shattering the process of representation and by curtailing the very
idea of repetition. Artaud's theatrical spectacles would be unique
gestural events with an immediate impact. The fierce edge of provocation and imminent disaster in Artaud's theatrical writings was
still compellingly present in 'No More Masterpieces': 'we see from
so many signs that all that which allowed us to live is no longer
holding out, that we are all mad, desperate and sick, and I invite *us
all* to react.'[60] Like his manifesto *The Theatre and Cruelty* of the
same year, this essay was not published until 1938. By the time 'No
More Masterpieces' appeared, Artaud had staged only one unique
spectacle and had abandoned written language. He himself had
fallen into a catastrophic state with his asylum internment of 1937.
In 'No More Masterpieces', Artaud wrote: 'We are not free. And
the sky can still fall on our heads. And the theatre is first of all made
to teach us that.'[61]

For Artaud, 1934 was a year of inaction and lassitude. He had
stopped writing the essays that anticipated and delineated his
Theatre of Cruelty, and now put all his efforts into arranging a
spectacle. But all his work led him into relentlessly repeated dead-
ends in 1934; only his stubborn determination not to let go of the
Theatre of Cruelty pulled him through. He left the Villa Seurat and
spent much of the year moving around hotels in Montparnasse,
although in the middle of the year his financial situation necess-
itated a temporary return to his mother's flat. Early in January,
Artaud gave a reading to generate funding for the Theatre of
Cruelty at the home of a wealthy socialite poetess, Lise Deharme, in
front of an audience of financiers. He had promised Lise Deharme
– who would become a source of great fury for Artaud three years
later – that a short article he had written on her poetry would

appear in *La Nouvelle Revue Française* to coincide with the reading. Paulhan left the article out of the January issue, and this caused Artaud embarrassment. He had hoped that Lise Deharme would herself fund his theatre. He was now reconciled to having to stage a compromised, textual spectacle before he could undertake his true work. At the reading he performed *Richard II* by Shakespeare (whose work he detested), as well as his own scenario of the previous year, *The Conquest of Mexico*. Artaud's hostility towards the financiers was barely hidden, and no substantial funding resulted from the reading. He was searching for other plays that would be more suitable for his aims than Shakespeare, and he was briefly attracted to *The Château of Valmore*, a story by the Marquis de Sade adapted for the theatre by Pierre Klossowski. He also wrote a play himself, *The Torture of Tantalus*, based on a Greek tragedy. His plan for *The Torture of Tantalus* was to stage it in a factory in his home-town of Marseilles, and he made a journey there in mid-May 1934 to discuss the project with a factory owner. But delays and financial problems came up, and Artaud abandoned that option. Later in the year, he tried to borrow Charles Dullin's theatre in Paris to stage his play, and that project also collapsed.

In the first months of 1934, Artaud became close friends with Pierre Klossowski's brother, the twenty-six-year-old painter Balthus. The two men were strikingly similar in physical and facial appearance, although Artaud was twelve years senior. Balthus gave Artaud great encouragement for his theatre at this difficult point in its development. In turn, Artaud wrote an article about Balthus's exhibition at the Galerie Pierre in Paris in May 1934; he emphasized the 'violent inspiration'[62] layered in Balthus's technically meticulous paintings, which projected an aura of hallucinatory eroticism. Artaud visited Balthus every evening during this period. On one occasion, he found Balthus in a coma after attempting suicide with an overdose of laudanum. Balthus had placed a photograph of his lover by his bed, and the obvious allusion appalled Artaud, for whom only the theatre would have been a matter for suicide at this time. Balthus survived to collaborate with Artaud in the following year.

In June Artaud had to take another film role, arranged by one of his film-producer cousins, Alexandre Nalpas. He travelled to Algeria to play the part of the teeth-grinding emir Abd-el-Kader in the military comedy *Sidonie Panache*. Artaud considered it a particularly degrading experience. He disliked growing a beard for the role, having always been clean-shaven. Not a lover of physical exercise, he was also required to ride around on a horse. The shooting of the film lasted from mid-June to mid-July. Artaud stayed at Laghouat, on the edge of the Sahara desert, and the landscape there made a deep impression upon him: 'Europe is far away, the civilized West has disappeared, and the true desert stretches out, excoriated, washed right to the bone, sifted molecule by molecule, naked, obscene, fearsome and menacing, obscene because it is without shame, with a cruel sensuality, meticulously naked.'[63] Two years later, he would experience the landscape of Mexico with a similarly strong and vivid fascination. Soon after his return from Algeria, Artaud was hired to add his voice to the truncated sound version of *Napoleon* which Abel Gance was preparing. It was now eight years since Artaud had played Marat in the original silent film. His cries and exclamations in the sound version are passionate and powerful, but are also wildly out of synchronization with Marat's lip-movements. (One factor in this may have been Artaud's distaste for the process of dubbing, which he had attacked in one of his essays on the cinema.)

Having made some money, Artaud was able to take a short holiday in Saint-Tropez in September, but this was followed by another detoxification treatment, at the Jeanne d'Arc clinic in the south-east of Paris. (It was the same clinic where Carl Theodor Dreyer had gone to recuperate after shooting his film *The Passion of Joan of Arc*, in which Artaud appeared.) A new treatment of injections was tried on Artaud, but it failed to prove effective. Later in the month, he wrote two short texts articulating the enclosure and desperation he felt in the face of his drug addiction:

> If I stop taking drugs, that means death. I mean that only death can cure me of the infernal palliative of drugs, from which only a precisely calculated absence, not too long in duration, allows me to be what I am . . . I can do nothing with opium, which is certainly the most abominable deception, the most fearsome invention of the void which has ever impregnated human sensibilities. But at any given moment I can do nothing without this culture of the void inside me.[64]

On 2 December 1934 Artaud wrote to the publisher of *La Nouvelle Revue Française*, Gaston Gallimard, announcing that he wanted to collect all his theatre essays into a book. Gallimard was one of the most prestigious French publishers. At this point,

Artaud was suggesting the title *The Theatre and the Plague* for his book. He wrote: 'The publication of these texts seems appropriate to me since in them I formulate the theory of a new theatre, for a world which is necessarily going to change, and since it appears to me that the moment has come to abandon theory and go on to actions.'[65] Although he had revised *The Theatre and the Plague* for its appearance in *La Nouvelle Revue Française* in October 1934, it was now a year since the last of these theatre essays had been written. Many more delays would occur before the book was finally published as *The Theatre and its Double* (Artaud discovered this new title during his voyage to Mexico in January 1936). Gallimard originally rejected Artaud's proposal, in February 1935, and it was not until February 1938 that he published the book in an edition of only 400 copies. Artaud was then at the asylum of Sotteville-lès-Rouen. A new edition of 1,525 copies appeared in 1944, by which time Artaud was interned at Rodez. The book then went out of print for twenty years, until it reappeared in 1964 as the fourth volume of Artaud's *Collected Works* in French. It was soon translated into many languages, including English, and exercised a huge inspirational – rather than technical – influence on European and American theatre. Among the most exceptional of the many practitioners of Artaud's ideas have been the Polish director Jerzy Grotowski with his 'Theatre Laboratory', and the New York director Julian Beck. Beck's 'Living Theatre' company (which included Al Pacino and Richard Gere) also worked in South America, France and Italy; Beck wrote of Artaud's profound impact upon him in his book *The Life of the Theatre*. Beck's theatre company was a provocative and vocal group with revolutionary aims; it intended to shatter both performance and social boundaries. (Beck had the same financial problems as Artaud in maintaining his company; shortly before his death in 1985, he was making film appearances as the cadaverous villain in *Poltergeist II* and alongside Mickey Rourke in *9½ Weeks*.) It was through the distorting intermediary of the Living Theatre that the influence of Artaud's work entered the field of rock music at the end of the 1960s. Jim Morrison of The Doors attempted to incorporate elements from *The Theatre and its Double* into his performances. More recently, experimental musicians such as Blixa Bargeld of the Berlin group Einstürzende Neubaten have been attracted to the movement towards violent fragmentation in Artaud's work.

Finally, in 1935, Artaud was able to stage the theatrical spectacle he had been working towards for so long. His only other project during the first half of 1935 was the writing of notes towards a soon-abandoned book entitled *Satan* (for which Gallimard offered him a contract). Artaud began the year by writing a second play, *The Cenci*, completing it early in February. He was enthusiastic about this new tragedy, and gave a reading of it to a number of literary figures including Gide. Artaud considered that his play reached 'the last degree of violence'.[66] The tragedy was drawn from two sources: a document translated from the Italian by Stendhal in 1837, and a tragedy by Shelley dating from 1819, of which Artaud had been aware at least since 1931. Cenci was a sixteenth-century Italian count; he was tried for sodomy and imprisoned three times. An atheist, he constantly had to appeal for the Pope to pardon his excesses. He hated his children, and raped his daughter Beatrice. Two of Cenci's servants murdered him by driving nails into his throat and one of his eyes. Beatrice was tortured and executed for her part in the murder of her father.

Artaud's own presence in his play was unmistakable. Cenci pro-poses a war against the Pope – as Artaud had with his Surrealist open letter to the Pope in 1925 – and he is given a speech which comes almost directly from 'No More Masterpieces': 'Free? When the sky is ready to fall on our heads, who can dare to talk to me about freedom?'[67] Count Cenci was the role which Artaud had earmarked for himself, but his tragedy was a flawed and com-promised vehicle for his ideas. Although gesture, lighting and noise would work to give it life on the stage, the play was fatally textual and bound to the conventional theatre. It was the kind of play whose obliteration Artaud's manifestos had demanded. As the only spectacle which Artaud was to stage for the Theatre of Cruelty, *The Cenci* embodied the contradictions of his practical experiments in the theatre. His friend Roger Blin reports that Artaud considered his play 'a commercial piece, half-way to what he wanted to do in the theatre'.[68] Artaud himself admitted the inadequacy of *The Cenci* for his project: 'There will be between the Theatre of Cruelty and *The Cenci* the difference which exists between the roaring of a waterfall or the unleashing of a natural storm, and all that remains of their violence once it has been recorded in an image.'[69]

Artaud had written *The Cenci* with the rigour of his own theatre direction in mind, and he wanted to exert his control over all aspects of the spectacle. But the financial aspects of the production interfered with this desire. Through Balthus and the musicologist

Pierre Souvtchinsky, Artaud had met a rich Russian woman named Iya Abdy, who offered to finance the spectacle on the condition that she could play Beatrice Cenci. She had acted before, in Dullin's company, but Roger Blin believed she was far too old for the role. Artaud agreed to the condition. Robert Denoël also put some money into Artaud's project, and his wife took the part of Cenci's wife in the play. The only theatre available was completely unsuitable: the Folies-Wagram was traditionally constructed, and specialized in operetta. Again Artaud accepted, in order to maintain the momentum of his project. The performances were set to begin on 7 May 1935, and the rehearsals were held throughout April.

The young actor Jean-Louis Barrault had been given a role, but Barrault apparently quarrelled with Iya Abdy and walked out. Artaud also cast Roger Blin as one of Cenci's assassins. Blin, who had never acted before, was allowed to do his own make-up; he divided his face into quarters and painted them different colours. He also helped Artaud with the rehearsals, noting each character's movements with a different coloured crayon. The rehearsals went badly: Artaud's cast failed to understand what he was demanding of them. He made many literary allusions, and was aggressive. Balthus had designed the theatre set, and the composer Roger Désormière collected a number of sound effects, including factory noises for the scene in which Beatrice Cenci is tortured. For *The Cenci*, Désormière initiated the use of stereophonic sound in the theatre, and the volume of noise to be used was extremely loud.

Two weeks before the première of *The Cenci*, Artaud gave an interview declaring his desire for the audience to be 'plunged into a bath of fire'. He wanted the audience to participate 'with their souls and their nerves'.[70] By the end of the rehearsals, he was already exhausted from having to supervise the financial aspects of the production, as well as from directing the play and acting the leading role. His voice was cracking. The dress rehearsal was held on 6 May, and the gala première took place on 7 May. It was a fashionable social event, and princesses and counts patronized the spectacle. (The French Minister of Foreign Affairs, Pierre Laval, with whom Artaud was on friendly terms, also attended one of the performances.) In such a sympathetic atmosphere, the opening night went well; Artaud played Cenci with great ferocity and vocal agility. After the show, he was elated, and the cast went to the Coupole café to celebrate. But it soon became clear that one performance had burned out the spectacle. As the subsequent performances went on, problems accumulated. The many news-paper reviews were almost all hostile, and derided what they saw as a strange mixture of cacophony and strained gestures; financial difficulties arose with the low attendances; and Artaud's control over events was quickly disintegrating. He was working constantly on the production, and putting all the money he could generate into it, but he still had to worry about how to survive and pay his hotel bill. On 15 May, the situation at the Folies-Wagram became criti-cal, and Artaud wrote desperately to Paulhan for an advance on his book of theatre essays: 'Things are going badly and if I don't find a financial backing of fifteen thousand francs in twenty-four hours, we will have to stop . . . It would be a huge favour that you could do for me, right now, because I am really at the end of my powers and of my nervous resistance . . . I have made an immense effort and now I find myself in front of an abyss: this is the result.'[71] Some stop-gap money was found, but a few days later the problems escalated again. *The Cenci* closed on 21 May, after seventeen per-formances. The existence of the Theatre of Cruelty in the Parisian theatre was at an end.

3

Mexico, Brussels, Ireland

After the collapse of *The Cenci* as the embodiment of the Theatre of Cruelty, Artaud began a series of journeys that continued until September 1937, when he was put in a strait-jacket on a boat between Ireland and France. More than any other phase of Artaud's life, his journeys of 1936 and 1937 involve a headlong rush towards breakdown and silence. As such, they are crucial to Artaud's work, despite the fact that only a limited amount of writing emerged from them. He conducted an exhaustive probing and reformulation of culture on the trajectory of these journeys. Artaud travelled from Paris to Mexico City, on to the Sierra Tarahumara, and back to Paris; then to Brussels for another desolate, provocative performance; and finally to Ireland, to the Aran Islands on the western coast, to Dublin and his imprisonment there in Mountjoy Prison, and back to France and an asylum incarceration of almost nine years. These are journeys which move steadily more out of control, away from society and security. They were impelled by Artaud's constant yearning for a wild, apocalyptic force which would violently erase his humiliating experiences in the Parisian theatre, thereby resuscitating his dreams and his life. A profusion of strange images and signs in his work may be traced back to these profoundly exploratory journeys.

Artaud fled Paris in January 1936 for many reasons. He could no longer countenance a theatre which depended upon the fallibilities of an acting troupe, such as that which had performed *The Cenci*. Now, even more than when his association with the Surrealists and the Alfred Jarry Theatre had collapsed, he could not tolerate collaboration of any kind. His theatre would now take on huge proportions, and simultaneously be reduced to tortured physical substance. It would be both the savage landscape and lost rituals of Mexico and Ireland, and also Artaud's own body as it travelled through, interpreted and imaginatively reconstructed this barbarously grandiose theatre-in-flux. Moving towards the Sierra Tarahumara of Mexico, Artaud foresaw a new origin for his work in a

landscape of forbidding mountains which paralleled that around the
city of his birth, Marseilles.

Artaud anticipated that he would discover a revolutionary society
in Mexico, and that it would conform to his vision of a kind of
anatomical revolution which could dispense with its own history.
He believed that the Mexican revolution of 1910–11 had signalled a
return to the mythological concerns of the Indian civilizations
which had existed before the Spanish Conquest of 1519. He would
be the agent who could catalyse and focus these revolutionary
forces; voyaging across the Atlantic Ocean from Europe as the
Conquistadors had done over four hundred years earlier, he would
undo the damage they had exerted on the native Mexican civilizations and their rituals. Although Artaud was disappointed in his
attempt to break utterly from European society, he nevertheless
found in Mexico a tenable image of revolution, which fed into his
work until his death. He discovered revolution inscribed in the
Mexican landscape itself, as a perpetually self-cancelling and self-
creative force. And with the Tarahumara Indians, he participated
in rites of calamity and resuscitation which strengthened his concept of a physical revolution with the capacity to transform the
natural world. It was with the Tarahumara Indians that Artaud
took the hallucinogenic drug peyote, which was central to the
Indians' rituals. In this way, Artaud seized at a drug which was
bound into an entire mythology of destruction and revolution, and
which he took only during that one short period of his life. He later
wrote:

> I took peyote in the mountains of Mexico with the Tarahumaras,
> and I had a packet of it which lasted me for two or three days; I
> thought myself then, at that moment, to be living the happiest three
> days of my existence.
> I had stopped being bored, trying to find a reason for my life, and
> I had stopped having to carry my body around.
> I understand now that I was inventing life – that I was bored when
> I no longer had imagination, and that was what peyote gave to me.[1]

Artaud's short-lived use of peyote contrasts with the agonizing
relentlessness of his addiction to opium in Paris, and his attempts at
detoxification there.

The travels Artaud undertook from 1936 to 1937, to Mexico,
Brussels and Ireland, make up a self-willed catastrophic journey.
Rather than attempt to reverse the failure of *The Cenci* within the

context of the Parisian theatre, or to undertake a collaboration with a friend such as Jean-Louis Barrault, Artaud chose to put his life at stake, as raw material in the service of the colossal designs and dreams of his work. The resulting sequence of journeys is a terrible smash, with Artaud's body and mental faculties compacted into an instrument of exploration and, finally, disintegration.

In the period between the collapse of *The Cenci* on 21 May 1935 and his departure for Mexico on 6 January 1936, Artaud's life was frantic. The failure of the Theatre of Cruelty hit him hard, though he was able to work through some of his abandoned proposals at the end of his life, with his recordings and final performances of 1946–8. The journey to Mexico was formulated almost at the same time as the closing of *The Cenci*; it was a journey born of despair, postponed over the second half of 1935 only through a mass of financial troubles, which compounded Artaud's need to leave Paris behind. Thoughts of Mexico had been with him at least since January 1933, when his scenario *The Conquest of Mexico* – intended for the Theatre of Cruelty – had been completed. Tibet seems to have been an alternative which Artaud considered, but the journey to Mexico had the advantage that it would certainly prove exacting, in both physical and intellectual terms. And the crossing of the ocean signalled a tangible separation from what Artaud had suffered in Europe.

The manifestos and proposals for the Theatre of Cruelty now appeared to be amputated from their potential realization in the performance space. Nevertheless, Artaud continued to edit his collection for publication by Gallimard, and added several new texts. The collection had no set title at this point, as Artaud intended to find one during his coming voyage to Mexico. Two of the new texts, 'An Affective Athleticism' and 'The Theatre of Séraphin', were about the actor's gestures and respiratory capacities. They were written at a time when Artaud himself was in a state of physical inaction, his opium consumption having accelerated dangerously with the collapse of *The Cenci*. (His acting role in that play was to be the last he would ever take on in the theatre.) These two new theatre texts interpret the actor's breathing according to material drawn from the Cabbala and from Chinese acupuncture; Artaud's actor is one whose body can scream exhaustively, through a combination of respiratory elements. Artaud complains that 'Nobody knows how to scream anymore in Europe';[2] in

'The Theatre of Séraphin', he follows his own scream through its trajectory, using a language of spectacular and ferocious poetry:

> To scream I must fall.
> It is the scream of the thunderstruck warrior who, in a wild noise of mirrors, crushes the shattered walls in passing.
>
> I fall.
> I fall but I am not afraid.
> I throw out my fear in the noise of rage, in a solemn bellowing . . .
> But with this thunderstruck scream, to scream I must fall.
> I fall into an underworld and I cannot get out, I can never get out . . .
> And it is here that the cataracts begin.
> This scream that I have just thrown out *is* a dream.
> But a dream which eats the dream.[3]

Artaud also wrote an introductory text, 'Theatre and Culture', for his collection, reworking it after his return from Mexico. In this text he created vivid imagery of the gestural language which his theatre, and his concept of life itself, could project. The participants of both would be 'like torture victims who are being burned and who are making signs from the stake'.[4]

Jean-Louis Barrault, who was one of Artaud's closest friends during this period, proposed that they should collaborate on a theatrical production. Barrault, still in his mid-twenties, was becoming increasingly renowned as a theatre and film actor. The month after *The Cenci*, Barrault staged an adaptation of William Faulkner's novel *As I Lay Dying*, under the title *Around a Mother*, which was a great success. Among the cast was Génica Athanasiou. Artaud wrote an enthusiastic review of the piece for *La Nouvelle Revue Française*, and he included it in his collection of theatre essays. Such a collaboration might well have brought new life to Artaud's theatrical proposals. But he refused Barrault's offer: 'I DO NOT WANT that there could be, in a production directed by me, even a blink of the eye which does not belong to me . . . Finally I do not believe in associations, especially since Surrealism, because I no longer believe in the purity of men.'[5] (After his release from Rodez, Artaud was hostile to Barrault because he was still involved in the theatre.) Instead of the collaboration, Barrault had to be content with donating money towards the journey to Mexico. Artaud himself raised some money by making the final two appearances of his eleven-year film-acting career, which had foundered so dishearteningly since his glorious roles in *Napoleon* and *The Passion of Joan of Arc* during the mid-1920s. In *Lucrecia Borgia* – a historical melodrama by Abel Gance, shot between July and October 1935 – Artaud plays Savonarola and is burned at the stake (generating the imagery for 'Theatre and Culture'). His last role was as an eccentric chemist in Maurice Tourneur's dire costume drama *Koenigsmark*, shot between August and November 1935.

Artaud intended to visit Indian tribes and to participate in their rituals during his time in Mexico; for this, an official sanction from the French Government would be a considerable assistance. All through the second half of 1935 he went from department to department, suffering rejection – his letters of application were inappropriately seeped in an imagery of fire and magic – before finally being given approval for his journey by the Education Ministry. He wanted backing from a popular wide-circulation newspaper, such as *Paris-Soir*, so that he could send reports of his great mission back to France. But without more explicit government support and recognition for his journey, this project failed to materialize. In order to sustain his journey financially, Artaud planned to give a series of lectures in Mexico City, which could then be published by the Mexican press. This project did come to fruition: the Mexican public was avid for information about European literary fashions. In anticipation of these lectures, Artaud began to prepare material which reveals the expanse of the ambition he held for his journey, though it was already shadowed by a sense of disillusionment. He was now retrospectively conceiving of his Theatre of Cruelty as a parallel to the revolutionary flux of Mexican culture, and he aimed to find cultures in Mexico which would vindicate the proposals he had made for the theatre. These cultures would possess a fierce, specifically physical language, which could suck all other languages into itself and would exist independently, without the need for texts or for writing of any kind. Artaud was idealizing the Mexican Indians as the embodiment of these dreams about culture. He believed that the Indians would be silent beings, that their blood itself would be able to speak and communicate with immediacy. Artaud's expectations of Mexico were passionate and extreme; he was conscious that, after the failure of *The Cenci*, the literary milieu of Paris had begun to consider him a madman and to ostracize him. He believed that for the Mexicans, by contrast, 'the madman is in the true world, and the true, like death, does not scare them'.[6] He was ready to defend his Mexican project as a huge and inventive journey of dreaming: 'if you find all that fantastic, absurd, imaginary, and irrational, don't forget that I took care to say at the beginning of this dream that I was dreaming . . .'[7]

On 11 September 1935 Artaud began a detoxification cure at the Henri-Rousselle clinic, in preparation for his journey. He requested free treatment since he was unemployed and had no money. At this point he was regularly taking a dose of forty grammes of opium once every sixty hours (he generally absorbed it in the form of laudanum – a solution of opium in alcohol); his maximum dose was seventy grammes, and in the period since his last detoxification at the Henri-Rousselle clinic in 1932, he had also been taking heroin. The detoxification regime proved intolerable for Artaud; he left the clinic on 16 September, prematurely and against medical advice, as he had done in 1932.

During the final months before his departure, Artaud became attached to a young Belgian woman, Cécile Schramme, who would become a central figure in his life after his return from Mexico. Cécile Schramme was the friend of an eighteen-year-old painter and dancer named Sonia Mossé, with whom Artaud had a brief liaison at this time. Sonia Mossé's face is known from the many photographs taken of her by the Surrealist Man Ray. She was to be deported from Paris during the Second World War and die in a Nazi gas chamber; Artaud was interned at Rodez when he heard of this, and he drew a portrait in memory of her.

Artaud's last weeks in Paris were hectic. He made preparations for his journey and attempted to borrow more money. Through the intermediary of Roger Blin, Artaud became reconciled with André Breton, and invited him to a private reading of the play Artaud had written for the Theatre of Cruelty, *The Torture of Tantalus* (Artaud had written to his doctor at the Henri-Rousselle detoxification clinic: 'Opium is the torture of Tantalus.')[8] This reading, which Artaud gave on 15 November, was the last appearance he made before his departure. It appears that he took the only manuscript of his play with him to Mexico – perhaps with the intention of rewriting or even of staging it there – and that it was either lost or destroyed during the journey. Since his journey had government approval, Artaud was able to arrange a discount on his boat ticket to Mexico. He finally left Paris for the Belgian port of Antwerp on 6 January 1936.

The voyage to Mexico took almost a month. Artaud travelled on a large cargo vessel, the SS *Albertville*, which left Antwerp on 10

January. He used the isolation of the sea crossing as an opportunity
to detoxify himself. This self-imposed regime was more successful
than that imposed upon him four months earlier at the Henri-
Rousselle clinic. By the time he reached Mexico, Artaud could
declare that 'the man terribly hardened, and black with air and
light, is starting to manifest himself'.[11] On 25 January, while the
boat was docked for a short time at a small port in North America,
Artaud wrote to Jean Paulhan in Paris:

> I believe that I've found the right title for my book.
> It will be:
> THE THEATRE AND ITS DOUBLE
> since if theatre doubles life, life doubles the true theatre . . .
> This title responds to all the doubles of theatre which I believe I've
> found over so many years: metaphysics, plague, cruelty . . .
> And the Double of theatre is the real, *which is not used* by people
> today.[12]

The boat then turned south along the Atlantic coast towards Cuba,
reaching Havana on 30 January. Artaud made contact with several
Cuban artists and writers there, and left a number of writings
attacking European culture and humanism for publication in
Cuban newspapers. He also attended a voodoo ceremony, and was
given a little sword embedded with hooks by a Negro sorcerer. He
kept the sword throughout his Mexican journey, and by the time he
returned to Paris it had acquired an immense significance in his
eyes. The final stage of the sea voyage took Artaud to the Mexican
port of Veracruz, from where he caught a train inland towards
Mexico City on 7 February. Artaud had by now spent all the little
money he had, and arrived in the Mexican capital penniless.

The Mexico of 1936 was not the revolutionary country Artaud
had been anticipating. Although a number of artists, such as the
muralist Diego Rivera, were demanding that Indian culture should
be incorporated into the metropolitan culture (which was dominated by European influences), government persecution of the
Indians persisted. The suppression of their rituals – such as the
peyote dance – had continued since the Spanish Conquest. Mexican
mainstream culture ignored the aspects of the ancient Aztec civilization which made it so compelling for Artaud – factors such as the
interpenetration of violence and art, and the sense of catastrophe
which was integral to the Indians' view of nature and culture.
During the 1860s, France had furthered its colonial aspirations in

Mexico with the installation of a monarchy headed by Ferdinand Maximilian, who was chosen by the French Emperor Napoleon III; but in the face of opposition from the United States, the enterprise collapsed in 1867. The French left Mexico and Prince Maximilian was arrested and executed. Since the Revolution of 1910–11 and the overthrow of the longstanding dictator Pofirio Díaz, Mexico had been in a state of political turmoil. During the years 1930–31 there had been a surge of anti-Communism; this had stabilized under the rule of President Lazero Cardénas, which brought a swing to the Left in 1934. At the time Artaud was in Mexico, official harassment of the Catholic Church was still strong, and the intellectual life of the capital was dominated by groups of young Marxists. The aura of revolution which still clung to Mexico had attracted other writers, artists and film-makers from across the Atlantic, notably Sergei Eisenstein, who worked on his abandoned film *Que Viva Mexico!* there in 1931. Breton followed Artaud to Mexico in 1938. (Although Breton went to Mexico largely because he was in a perilous financial situation in Paris and was offered a lucrative lecture tour, he nevertheless exerted some impact on the artistic situation in Mexico; he stayed with Rivera and his wife Frida Kahlo, and collaborated with Leon Trotsky, who was in exile in Mexico and would be murdered there in 1940.)

Artaud's arrival in Mexico City caused something of a sensation. The fierce passion of his attitude towards Mexican culture communicated itself to the intellectuals of the capital. The writers and artists Artaud met during his first weeks in Mexico City did not sympathize wholeheartedly with his pro-Indian stance, and objected to his repudiation of Marxism; nevertheless, they were ready to hear all he had to say. Very quickly, a series of lectures at the Alliance Française and the University of Mexico was arranged, and Artaud began to publish his exhortations on Mexican culture in the government newspaper *El Nacional Revolucionario*. He attempted to develop a political language – neither of the Left nor of the Right, and even less of the Centre – for these writings. His rhetoric of revolution and artistic experimentation proved attractive to his audiences and readers. A major factor in his popularity was that the Mexican intellectual society wanted news of the latest French theatrical and literary successes, including Surrealism, and expected Artaud to provide this information. Artaud's principal aim was to visit the Indian tribes, and he was soon planning a journey to the remote lands of the Tarahumara Indians, but for a time he enjoyed the adulation he received in Mexico City. He was accustomed to his work being dismissed or ignored in the Parisian literary milieu; now, his newspaper articles were carrying his cultural dreams to an entire nation. However, this attention did not provide Artaud with sufficient funds to survive in Mexico City. He stayed in the houses of writers he had met, and began taking drugs again. He had to write to friends such as Paulhan and Balthus in Paris, appealing for them to send him money, and he was reduced to writing publicity material for a brewery.

The material Artaud delivered in lectures and published in newspapers ranged widely in content. On 18 March he gave a prestigious lecture at the Alliance Française, providing a purely informative account of developments in the French theatre over the past thirty years. He gave pride of place to his own Alfred Jarry Theatre (although the Theatre of Cruelty was absent from his account), and to actor friends such as Barrault. He also spoke of his quarrels with the Surrealists in the first of three lectures at the University of Mexico. But most of Artaud's pronouncements in Mexico City were inflammatory appeals for Mexican youth to abandon Marxism, and to embody a revolutionary movement that would turn back in time to before the Spanish Conquest. It would be a revolution of magic and anatomical metamorphosis. These incitements constituted a heightened version of Artaud's concept of revolution from the mid 1920s, when he had been involved in his dispute with Breton on the subject. With great intensity, Artaud was now imagining and evoking an anti-capitalist, anti-Marxist revolutionary culture, centred on the body and its perpetual will to obliterate societies and to reconstitute itself through creative acts. This was provocative in the context of the Mexican political situation of the time. Artaud claimed to be speaking from the position of discontented French youth (although, in fact, their concerns of 1936 were far from those of Artaud), to Mexican youth. For the only time in his life, Artaud's declarations turned against the individual as he demanded a universal culture based on an imagery of fire. His texts were translated from Artaud's French into Spanish at great speed, over café tables, by new friends such as José Ferrer and Luis Cordoza y Arágon. He lost his original manuscripts, and when the time came for these writings to be published in France, many of them had to be translated back from the Spanish. Artaud intended that his Mexican writings should be published as a collection, under the title *Revolutionary Messages*; but this did not happen during his lifetime.

All through the spring of 1936, Artaud tried to arrange his journey to visit an Indian tribe. He had chosen the Tarahumaras, who lived in the Sierra Madre region of northern Mexico, since he considered them to be uncontaminated by European civilization. They were also one of the few surviving tribes to base their rituals of magic and religion (they believed in many gods) on the drug peyote. Artaud's fascination with the peyote plant was directed towards the way in which the Indians used it to strengthen their mythological concept of the body's relationship with vital natural forces. Artaud had always relied upon opium as a way of constructing a barrier against the pain of his raw nerves; now, he turned to peyote as a means of attempting to shatter all barriers of perception, and as the agent which could obliterate the limits of time and space from which his Theatre of Cruelty spectacle had suffered. He was not the only writer of his generation to be drawn by the hallucinatory qualities of the drug: Henri Michaux and Aldous Huxley explored the visionary states generated by mescalin, a derivative of peyote.

The Tarahumaras had an utter disregard for material possessions which paralleled Artaud's own austerity. He owned no more than a suitcase of donated clothes and tattered manuscripts. And the Tarahumaras practised the only kind of communism which Artaud could tolerate:

> There exists, in the north of Mexico, a race of pure red Indians, the Tarahumaras. Forty thousand people live there, in a condition like that before the Flood. They are a challenge to this world where people talk so much of progress only because they have lost all hope of progressing.
>
> This race, which you would expect to be physically degenerate, has for over four hundred years resisted all that has come to attack it: civilization, interbreeding, Winter, war, wild animals, storm and forest. It lives naked in Winter, in mountains blocked by snow, contemptuous of all medical theories. Communism exists for this race through a feeling of spontaneous solidarity.
>
> Incredible though it may appear, the Tarahumara Indians live as though they were already dead . . . They do not see reality, and draw magical powers from the contempt which they hold towards civilization.[11]

Artaud was deeply moved by his time with the Tarahumaras. He was to rework what he had seen and experienced there throughout the rest of his life, completing his final text on the peyote dance only a fortnight before his death. And he used the Tarahumaras' ritual cries and gestures as a source for the screams of refusal which he performed in January 1948 for his recording *To have done with the judgement of god*.

Artaud believed that the experiences he was to bring back from the mountains would astound people in Paris; this would erase the humiliation which he had suffered with the failure of *The Cenci*. He wrote to Paulhan that '*I hope* to be able to tell you many stunning things on my return, which will show to everybody that the world is double and triple'.[12] He also wanted to bring back weapons from the Indians, to enable him to settle scores in Paris. He declared to Barrault:

> I must take revenge against many people, and many things. It is impossible for me not to take it. You must understand that I have a heavy heart, and that there are some dirty insults which I cannot forget . . .
> I intend to return fairly soon, in around 3 or 4 months, end of September, beginning of October. And I hope to be definitely armed at that moment.[13]

In part Artaud's anger was due to the obstacles that were delaying his departure for the Tarahumara mountains. As usual, these were of a financial nature. Finally he obtained approval from the Mexican Government to visit the Indians and research their behaviour for artistic ends. Many of the writers he had met in Mexico City signed a petition to the President in Artaud's favour, and all the expenses of the journey were to be met by the Mexican Government. Artaud regarded his departure with triumph and determination: 'I leave in search of the impossible. Even so, we will see if I am able to find it.'[14] Towards the end of August 1936 he took the train from Mexico City, travelling one thousand kilometres to Chihuahua, the nearest city to the Sierra Tarahumara; from there he continued on horseback into the mountainous region. Before confronting the Indians' drug, he wanted to be rid of the drugs which tied him to his European addiction, and so he threw away the last of his heroin at the base of the mountains.

It took Artaud five or six days on horseback to reach the Tarahumara village of Norogachic, at an altitude of six thousand metres. The sudden lack of heroin caused him agony. His guide had to help Artaud on to his horse, put his hands on the reins, and close his fingers around them. In extremely hot and stormy weather, Artaud and his guide passed through villages of poor, diseased Indians who ignored their pleas for information about the peyote rite. Artaud's condition was increasingly precarious: 'On the fifth day, I believed I was entering hell. I was seeing red, literally, and it seemed to me that the road was burning.'[15] Along the roadside he saw groups of Indians masturbating, and assumed that they were trying to bewitch him and make him turn back. The Indians were hostile towards all white men. From the time of the Spanish Conquest onward, the white men had passed on disease and had tried to prevent the Indians from celebrating their drug rites. Artaud perceived the landscape around him as inscribed with numbers, letters and symbols; the rocks were twisted into a breathing, tortured configuration. It seemed to him that the entire landscape was alive, bursting with a language of magical immediacy that transmitted nature in a raw state of catastrophe and sexuality.

When he reached Norogachic, Artaud set about convincing the Indians that he wanted to participate in their peyote rite rather than suppress it. The Indians were suspicious, and angry that the Mexican Government's soldiers had recently destroyed a field of peyote. During the five weeks of Artaud's stay with the Tarahumaras, he managed to win their confidence. He stayed in the house of the region's government representative, who was also the local school-teacher. While waiting for the opportunity to witness the peyote rite, Artaud wrote articles on the Tarahumaras' culture to send to the newspaper *El Nacional Revolucionario* in Mexico City; many of his writings of this time were subsequently lost. Artaud believed that the Indians no longer understood their own rituals, and his anticipation of the peyote dance was already shadowed by disillusionment: 'I certainly needed some willpower to believe that something was going to happen. And all this, for what? For a dance, for a rite of some lost Indians who no longer even knew who they were nor where they came from, and who, when I questioned them, replied by telling stories of which they had lost the thread and the secret.'[16] For four weeks, Artaud tried to persuade the school-teacher that the Indians should be free to perform their ritual. Since Artaud had the backing of the Government, the school-teacher finally consented. One of the Indians had recently died, and so a special peyote rite could be held in his honour. But, as though to taunt Artaud, the Indians made elaborate preparations for the rite, so delaying it by a further week.

Over the next twelve years, Artaud was to give many accounts of what he witnessed during the all-night ritual of the peyote dance. All his accounts convey the impression of a fragmentary experience; he was certainly ill and exhausted at the time of the rite. The Indians believed that peyote broke time and gave them an infinite memory, but drinking the distilled peyote seems to have stopped Artaud's hallucinations rather than to have provoked new ones. At Rodez, he would say that he was not given a sufficient quantity of peyote by the chief sorcerer to be certain what its effects upon him were. His involvement in the peyote dance was undercut by the sense that his huge exertions in reaching the Tarahumaras had not been worth it, and he would not find a response to his vision of a revolutionary culture, nor a cure to his pain. The Tarahumaras believed that whatever advantage an outsider such as Artaud might draw from the rite would be something lost to them. Artaud's isolation at the heart of the rite made him still more intensely aware of the frailties of his own body: 'The physical hold was still there. This cataclysm which was my body . . . After twenty-eight days of waiting, I had still not come back into myself; – I should have said: left, into myself. Into myself, into this dislocated assemblage, this fragment of decayed geology.'[17] The rite generated a feeling of great fervour in Artaud, even great happiness. But it was also a time of sadness; he realized that his work had reached another dead-end. During his performance at the Vieux-Colombier theatre in January 1947, Artaud was to declare: 'In resorting to peyote I didn't want to enter a new world, but to leave a false world.'[18] The Indian sorcerers screamed and gestured at Artaud as he drank the peyote and then, as the rite demanded, spat the residue into a hole in the earth. He was at the point of collapse. His perception of the rite – the terrible constant noise of cries, beatings, stampings, and the bloodshed as a sorcerer cut his own flesh and dipped a horseshoe in the wound – oscillated between a belief that he was participating in an act of healing, and that what he saw was apocalyptic. The sun was to be killed when it rose at the end of the night's dancing, and a perpetual black night would be instituted in a negative rite of fire and catastrophic destruction. Artaud wrote: 'No, the sun will not come back.'[19]

After this draining experience, Artaud soon left the Tarahumaras. On 7 October he was back in Chihuahua. He wrote to Paulhan to ask if *The Theatre and its Double* had been published in France yet, but made no reference at all to the peyote rite in which he had just participated. When he arrived in Mexico City, Artaud began raising money for the journey back to Paris. He was eager to return to France as quickly as possible, and to see Cécile Schramme again. On 31 October, at Veracruz, he caught the steamship *Mexico*, which sailed directly to the port of Saint-Nazaire. Artaud arrived back in Paris in mid-November; he had been away from France for over ten months.

Artaud's return to Paris provoked no great interest in literary circles. While the failure attached to *The Cenci* had now receded into some oblivion, only a restrained appreciation was generated by Artaud's Mexican adventure. Paulhan agreed to publish some of Artaud's writings on the Tarahumaras in *La Nouvelle Revue Française*, and Artaud finally signed a contract with Gallimard for *The Theatre and its Double*. But life in Paris forcefully brought back the two overriding obstacles to Artaud's work – opium and poverty. He slept in the apartment of a friend, Jean-Marie Conty, during his first months back in Paris, and had to beg his friend from the Surrealist era, Robert Desnos, to give him radio work of any kind, even small roles or readings. Desnos suggested that Artaud should instead act in a film to make some money, but Artaud considered that impossible, believing that his physical condition was now too fragile. He was obsessed by his desire to execute a great, all-consuming work which would finally put him in control of his destiny, but he had no theatre, no materials, and no collaborators. He desperately wanted to continue to create, and this forced the emphasis of his work more deeply and relentlessly into his own body, so that it was scraped along behind the driving momentum of his derailed work.

Artaud was severely short of money – he went for days without eating, and spent his time sitting in the Dôme café on the boulevard du Montparnasse, where his friends had to pay for his drinks. He regularly insulted passers-by in the street. His consumption of opium was at such a dangerous level that Paulhan arranged for Artaud to receive an emergency payment from a writers' fund at the end of January 1937, so that he could undergo a detoxification cure. The stay at the clinic, in the rue Boileau, lasted from 25 February to 4 March, and proved as painful and futile as all the previous cures. Despite Artaud's determination to stop taking drugs and to marshall his forces towards the accomplishment of the next stage of his work, he began immediately to rely upon opium again after he left the clinic. In April he had to take a new detoxification cure, this time at a private clinic at Sceaux, on the southern outskirts of Paris.

1 Portrait photograph of Artaud by Man Ray, 1926

2 Artaud acting in his first film, Claude Autant-Lara's *Faits Divers*, 1924

3 Artaud acting in Raymond Bernard's 'abominable' war melodrama, *Les Croix du Bois*, 1931

4 Artaud on his arrival at the asylum of Rodez, 1943, shortly before the electroshock treatments

5 Artaud near the end of his life, Paris, 1948

6 Self-portrait drawing by Artaud
with outstretched hand and a
'death's head' at his shoulder, 1947

7 *The Projection of the True Body*, drawing by Artaud depicting his body before
(left) and after (right) his death, 1947–8

Paulhan paid the expenses anonymously, and Artaud was kept in complete solitude at his own request, with more successful results. On being discharged from the clinic, Artaud went to stay in the studio of a painter named René Thomas in the rue Daguerre, near the Montparnasse cemetery. It was a meeting place for many artists and writers, and those with nowhere else to stay were welcome there. Artaud's friend Anie Besnard was also living in the studio. During this period Artaud was given an ancient knotted cane by the wife of a Dutch painter named Kristians Tonny; she claimed that it had belonged to Saint Patrick in Ireland. It was an impressive object, and Artaud became hugely attached to it. Like the sword which he had been given in Cuba, the cane became both a weapon of violence and a sign of sexual vulnerability. Artaud began to carry it constantly, and when friends admired the cane and tried to touch it, he became enraged, complaining that it was as if they had grabbed at his penis. On one occasion he chased the former Dada leader Tristan Tzara around the place Saint Germain-des-Prés for touching the cane. He took it to a blacksmith and had a metal tip welded on to its end: when he walked along the boulevards striking the cane against the ground, it shot out sparks behind him.

Since his return from Mexico, Artaud had been seeing Cécile Schramme again. Their affair was volatile and heated. As Artaud's life became more and more precarious, he relied increasingly upon Cécile Schramme for a point of stability. He wrote to her:

> I love you
> because you have revealed human happiness to me.[20]

But Cécile Schramme was also a drug addict, and her promiscuity horrified Artaud. His ideas of sexuality had been in turmoil since the journey to Mexico, and he was preoccupied with a notion of pure physical will. When they were in bed together at night, he put the cane between them so that their bodies could not touch. Artaud's attitude towards Cécile Schramme fluctuated wildly – at times he was bitterly imperious, at other times extremely tender. While he was away from her during his detoxification cure of February–March, he asked her to draw signs that he had seen in the Tarahumaras' landscape – attempting to transfer that natural immediacy into his domestic Parisian landscape. In the spring of 1937 Artaud asked Cécile Schramme to marry him. After his release from the clinic at Sceaux he wanted to leave Paris again, and accepted an invitation from the writer Robert Poulet to give a lecture at the Maison d'Art in Brussels, where Cécile Schramme's parents lived. Artaud and Cécile Schramme made the journey to Brussels together around 14 May, so that Artaud could meet his future parents-in-law, and deliver his prestigious lecture.

The trip was a disaster. Cécile Schramme's father was the director of the Brussels tramway system, and he expected the forty-year-old Artaud to be able to provide substantial guarantees that he could support his daughter financially. Artaud had absolutely nothing to offer. His lecture took place at the Maison d'Art on 18 May. Its subject had been announced as 'the decomposition of Paris', and it attracted a cultured audience. But Artaud's lecture was to transform itself into another of the outrageous, invective events that stretch from his lecture on plague at the Sorbonne in 1933 to his final performance at the Vieux-Colombier in 1947. Artaud immediately announced that he had abandoned his prepared text. He then spoke about his journey to Mexico, his voice and gestures becoming increasingly hostile and violent. He also dealt with the effects of masturbation on the behaviour of Jesuit priests, thereby causing a large part of his scandalized audience to leave the hall, as had happened at the Sorbonne four years previously. At the close of his lecture, Artaud screamed and told the remnants of his audience: 'In revealing all this to you, I have perhaps *killed* myself!' The general outrage he created in Brussels was slight, since the newspapers did not report the performance. But it compounded the dissatisfaction of Cécile Schramme's parents, and the project of marriage was terminated. Although Artaud returned to Paris hurt and bewildered, he was also delighted at his lecture's impact upon its audience. For some weeks he defensively claimed to his friends that the marriage was still on, but that it would be delayed since Cécile was ill. Cécile Schramme remained a great focus of Artaud's affections and imagination. During his time at Rodez, he appointed her as one of his 'daughters of the heart', unlike Génica Athanasiou. He also tried to make contact with Cécile Schramme at the end of his time at Rodez, instructing his friends to find out where she was living. They found her at a sanatorium in Belgium, paralysed and prematurely aged by her drug abuse. She wanted nothing more to do with Artaud. She was to die in 1950, only two years after Artaud.

The time between Artaud's return from Brussels around 20 May 1937 and his departure for Ireland on 12 August was an exceptional period of his life in Paris. Following the effective detoxification at

Sceaux, he was taking no drugs at all. (An additional factor may well have been that he simply could not afford to buy any drugs.) His writings were consequently imbued with an extraordinary lucidity and a sense of determination. He began staying at René Thomas's studio again, and abandoned many of his manuscripts there. He also spent a great deal of time out on the streets and in the Dôme café. By the early summer months, he was sleeping out at night and begging on the boulevard du Montparnasse. He had recently written a magazine article on the Tarahumaras, entitled 'The Race of Lost Men', in which he described their style of begging in the Mexican cities. They displayed an attitude of 'supreme contempt. They had an air of saying: "Since you are rich, you are a dog, I am worth more than you, I spit on you."'[21] His cane remained with him at all times. He maintained contact with only a few people at this point of extreme preoccupation and isolation in his life. He was seeing the painter Sonia Mossé again, and complained that she would not tell him that she loved him because he refused to have sex with her. He met Breton frequently and also sent him numerous letters, prophesying an imminent upheaval that would lead to terrible calamities and finally to the end of the world. His statements were calm, purposeful and collected. For Artaud, this was a time of apocalyptic optimism. His letters were dense with imagery of fire. Breton was one of the few people who gave Artaud money and food during this period; despite his profound divergence from Breton in matters such as revolution and art, Artaud remained grateful until the end of his life for this material support. Artaud also became attached to Breton's daughter Jacqueline, whom he regarded as a radiant 'true sun' – the counter-weight to the Tarahumaras' dead black sun. In July, he met a young journalist named Anne Manson who had been recommended to speak to Artaud, since she was to be sent to Mexico as a correspondent. During their brief relationship, Artaud became fier-cely protective and sexually jealous. His attitude towards Anne Manson was deeply contradictory. While magisterially chiding her for her open sexuality, he praised and clung to what he saw as her asexual 'rare light', in the face of the final dark journey that he was now starting to contemplate. He wrote to her: 'It is best that I warn you that I am *certainly* a dangerous man, because I fear nothing and I *have no fear of losing*.'[22]

After his return from Mexico, Artaud had become fascinated by tarot cards and the predictions he could make with them. An

occultist named Manuel Cano de Castro instructed Artaud in the
workings of the tarot pack, although Artaud's interpretations were
always highly individual and served only to validate and intensify
his relentless preoccupation with imminent catastrophe. While
Artaud's interest in the tarot was short-lived, it fed into the creation
of the last text he wrote before his asylum internment, a poetic
prophecy entitled *The New Revelations of Being*. The text was
written around June 1937, soon after Artaud's break with Cécile
Schramme. On one level it recapitulated the collapse of their relationship as a narrative of terminal separation, treachery, exile and
apocalypse. Artaud projected his anger and hurt on to an inter-
continental level; according to his prophecy, he would emerge as a
figure with authoritarian and revelatory power over the world. His
writing was still utterly disciplined and poetically incisive:

> I say what I have seen and what I believe; and whoever says that I
> have not seen what I have seen, I will now tear off his head.
> For I am an unpardonable Brute, and it will be so until Time is no
> longer time . . .
> It is a true Desperate One who is speaking to you, and who never
> knew the happiness of being in the world until now that he has left
> this world, and is absolutely separated from it.[23]

In *The New Revelations of Being*, Artaud demanded a 'reclassing of
all values'. It would be 'fundamental, absolute, terrible', with a
more far-reaching and revolutionary scope than the one he had been
planning at the Surrealist Research Centre in 1925. Artaud foresaw
the emergence of an autocratic director of world events, whose
power would be forged from cataclysmic natural forces. At Rodez,
in 1943, he would point out a parallel between this and the rise of
Hitler. But in *The New Revelations of Being* it is explicitly Artaud
himself who directs the global upheaval by wielding his sword and
cane. After being dismissed as a fool and a madman, he passes
through physical trials, solitude and desperation to assume his new
identity as 'THE REVEALED ONE'. Artaud gives precise dates, very
close in the future, for the transformation and destruction he
anticipates:

> On the 7th [September, 1937], the door of the Infinite is open for
> the man. The tortured one is finally prepared. He can enter, he is at
> the same level as his work. He can begin.

> The 3rd of November, the Destruction is illuminated.

The 7th, it explodes in lightning.
The Tortured One has become for all the world the Recognized One,
THE REVEALED ONE.[24]

The text was published as a pamphlet by Robert Denoël at the end
of July, without the author's name. Artaud now desired to be pure
corporeal force, welded to the trajectory of his work, and to erase all
identifications with his past life. He also instructed Paulhan to
suppress the author's name from the publication of his text on the
Tarahumaras which appeared in *La Nouvelle Revue Française* on 1
August.

It was the cane which had reputedly belonged to Saint Patrick
that largely motivated Artaud's final journey, to Ireland. He
decided that he would return the cane to the Irish, to awaken them
to his appeals for revolution. He was calmly aware that it would be
his last journey, and announced it as such to his friends. He was to
leave Paris, as the scene of his humiliations, to confront what he
viewed as another wild and uncivilized landscape – the islands off
the western coast of Ireland. There, he would watch his prophecy
materialize. He left Paris abruptly and took a boat to Ireland,
arriving at the port of Cobh on 14 August. When he finally returned
to Paris, it was to be as an inmate of the Sainte-Anne asylum.

Artaud's journey to Ireland accumulated towards a point of
breakdown. While his sense of purpose and his need to correspond
with friends in Paris remained intact almost until his arrest, everything else in his life disintegrated beneath him. His exhaustive
interrogation of his own identity proved destabilizing, and finally
all-consuming. He became obsessed with real and imaginary
betrayals by the people he had been involved with in Paris. His
growing concern with religious ritual, which had its axis in the cane
and sword he carried with him to Ireland, fluctuated dangerously
between the kind of invective denunciation he had made during his
Brussels lecture, and an extreme piety which resonated, violently
distorted, from his religious schooling. Although this journey to
Ireland was to prove less testing physically than the journey to
Mexico of the previous year, its combination of traumatic self-
probings and violent attacks brought about Artaud's greatest
silence, which was to last for many years.

Artaud began his stay in Ireland like any other Parisian away for
the August holidays – by sending numerous postcards to his
friends. From Cobh, he crossed Ireland to the western coast.

Arriving in Galway, he took the boat to Inishmore, the largest of the Aran Islands. Inishmore possessed a spectacular barrenness which had attracted other writers to it, notably J. M. Synge; the documentary film-maker Robert Flaherty had visited the island in 1931, to make his film *Man of Aran*. Among the most imposing ancient constructions on Inishmore was the fortress Dun Aonghusa. Artaud headed for the most isolated regions of the island; he lodged with a local couple in a tiny village more than two hours' walk from Kilronan, the principal settlement on Inishmore. He was lucid and curious, complaining in a letter to Breton about how expensive the island was, and writing to Paulhan asking for money in order to extend his journey (perhaps north to Donegal, one of the major sites of the Saint Patrick legends). He also consulted a medium in Kilronan. He was still preoccupied with fire and destruction, and wrote to Breton that 'this time the end will burn up the means'.[25] Justifying his journey in a letter to his family, he wrote that he was searching for the 'last true descendant of the Druids', who would know that 'humanity must disappear by water and by fire'.[26] Artaud now had no money at all. Paulhan was seriously ill at the time, and in no position to help Artaud out as he had done during the journey to Mexico and in Paris. Artaud left the guest-house where he had been staying without paying his bill, attempting to reassure his hosts with a note written in English: 'I go to Galway *with the priest* to take money in Post office.'

Back in Galway on 2 September, Artaud booked into the Imperial Hotel. He stayed there for about a week. In his solitude, the preoccupations which had been developing on Inishmore now became stronger and more focused. He was still confident that the cataclysmic events he had foretold would soon begin to materialize (according to *The New Revelations of Being*, it was on 7 September that the 'tortured man' could begin his work). He wrote again to Breton, urging him to participate in these events. As at other times of extreme crisis in his life, when he was appealing for Breton's help or support, Artaud undercut his appeal with a rebuke levelled against Breton's political involvements. He wrote: 'I have always suffered from seeing you submitting, you, Breton, to structures, to rules and to Human denominations which manifest themselves in Systems, Doctrines and Parties.'[27] (Artaud's expulsion from the Surrealist movement, partly on political grounds, remained a source of anomisity for the rest of his life.) Artaud was convinced that society would attempt to suppress and silence him because of

the determinedly apocalyptic nature of his Irish mission. He expected to be arrested and imprisoned. He told Breton that this would
not be a cause for concern; he would shortly emerge with a transformed identity and a new name. The cane was still one of Artaud's
principal preoccupations. He imagined his work as that of an
isolated, Christ-like figure; for Artaud at this time, Christ was a
destructive figure, 'the Negative of Creation'.[28] In a letter to
Breton, he wrote: 'The christ was a magician who fought against
demons in the desert with a cane. And a stain of his own blood
stayed on this cane.'[29] From such letters, it seems certain that by
this time Artaud was experiencing hallucinations in which he was
assaulted sexually by malicious, demonic figures; these hallucinations would stay with him to the end of his life. He had to
struggle, scream and dance to protect himself from the assaults of
these nocturnal figures.

From Galway, Artaud wrote a detailed letter to Paulhan about
the advance due for *The Theatre and its Double*, which still had not
been published. But as the days there went on, he grew increasingly
exasperated and furious. The imminence of his prophecy was
leaking away. In reaction to a letter from Anne Manson about her
recent games of tennis and her desire to be in Mexico, Artaud raged
that such concerns were futile when 'modern life is made up of
homeless people starving to death, madmen, maniacs, imbeciles
and people made desperate by the errors of modern life'.[30] His
overwhelming fury was reserved for Lise Deharme, the rich
socialite at whose home Artaud had given the reading of his play
The Torture of Tantalus in November 1935. They had had an
argument before Artaud's departure for Ireland in which he had
attacked her political sympathies for the Left; she had responded
by accusing Artaud of being a ham actor, and by saying that he
should be burned as a sorcerer for believing in many gods (as the
Tarahumaras did). Now Artaud retaliated at a distance by sending
her death threats, via Breton, and by designing the first in a long
series of what Artaud called his 'spells'. These were pieces of paper
on which he wrote curses (and later, words of protection) in
brightly coloured inks, surrounded by symbolic drawings. He then
attacked the paper, tearing it and burning it with cigarettes, with
the intention of simultaneously inflicting wounds on the body of the
recipient.

On 8 September, Artaud left Galway for Dublin. He wrote: 'I am
going towards my Destiny.'[31] Again he failed to pay his hotel bill.

In Dublin, even without money and with little command of English, he managed to find a room in a boarding-house. He continued to write many letters to his friends in Paris; these reveal the fevered pitch of Artaud's thinking. He constantly battered at his obsessions. No longer calm, he was heading for a state of collapse. During his first two weeks in Dublin, Artaud determinedly reformulated his identity; any mention of his precarious material circumstances is entirely absent from the letters he wrote at this time. He declared to Anne Manson: 'Pushed by gigantic forces, I have finished by discovering *who* I am and by accepting what I am.'[32] For Artaud, cruelty was now a self-directed force of upheaval, conceived and executed in solitude; this force could also be imposed upon the external world whenever necessary. The humiliation of his broken relationship with Cécile Schramme still haunted Artaud; he wrote repeatedly to Anie Besnard, insisting that she must obliterate the memory of his marriage project. The ridicule he had suffered at the hands of the Parisian literary society continued to be a source of great hurt. He believed that Anne Manson would betray him to that milieu by revealing his whereabouts, which he desperately wanted to keep secret. He told Breton that the Anti-Christ was a customer of the Deux Magots café on the boulevard Saint Germain; it seems he was thinking of a friend of Breton's daughter Jacqueline, since he sent her one of his 'spells' to protect her from this man. This action may well have been motivated by jealousy. Artaud planned that Jacqueline Breton would be the wife of his new identity: 'You will be revenged, my dear Jacqueline, and also the Superior Being of whom *you are* the Predestined Wife.'[33] Artaud's religious preoccupations were now violent – the cruel Christ who wielded the cane would order the execution of the Pope. Artaud believed that the cane could still precipitate the end of the world; England would be among the first places to sink into the sea. And the power he commanded as the 'Enraged One' would soon give Artaud the right to speak with the voice of God. Always acutely conscious that what he said would be treated as mad or hilarious, Artaud pleaded in all his letters to be believed. He wrote: 'here is what must be understood: it's that the *Unbelievable*, yes, the Unbelievable – it's the Unbelievable which is the truth.'[34] With a final appeal to Jacqueline Breton on 21 September, Artaud abruptly fell silent.

Several days earlier, he had begun to provoke incidents in the Dublin streets. Crowds gathered around him as he brandished his cane and incited the people to act with him. On a number of occasions the Irish police intervened, but Artaud initially escaped arrest. At his Vieux-Colombier lecture ten years later, he would recall a beating he received during one of these incidents. He gave the exact time as three in the afternoon of 18 September, and stated that he suffered 'a blow from an agent provocateur with an iron bar, which snapped the vertebral column in two – twenty doctors have verified and examined the scar and the lesion.'[35] He remembered striking a police officer with his cane. Artaud believed that the English police wanted to prevent him from giving the cane back to the Irish people, for whom he still had some regard at this point. It seems he was searching for the right place to deposit the cane, and he visited the Dublin Museum and St Patrick's Cathedral. But on 20 September things began to go severely wrong. He was turned out into the street since he could not pay for his room. He tried to find refuge at the Jesuit College, and when he was refused admittance, he shouted and screamed. The police were called and fighting ensued. It was then that Artaud's cane disappeared. He would say at Rodez that he left it in a bed at the night-shelter where he then went to stay. (A likely alternative would be that the police confiscated it.) By this point, he was becoming disillusioned with the cane:

> I only used the cane in Ireland to impose silence upon the dogs that were after me, and the only reason I was put in prison and deported was because I myself realized that it was worthless as a means of defence and that I was becoming very bad, I mean more inept, idiotic and insipid in the soul each time I used it.[36]

He remained free for several more days, sleeping at the night-shelter. On 23 September he was arrested for vagrancy, and spent six days in Mountjoy Prison.

Artaud was deported as an 'undesirable', since he was in an unstable condition and had no money. The French consulate in Dublin arranged for him to be sent back to France on a steamship, the *Washington*. Before he left prison, his Cuban sword was returned to him. He was taken back to Cobh by two policemen, and sailed from there on 29 September. During the course of the voyage, two crewmen came into Artaud's cabin with a monkey wrench, ostensibly to do maintenance work. (Alternatively, they may have wished to threaten Artaud for making too much noise.) He attacked them. At Rodez in 1945, Artaud recounted the sequence of events:

I was interned at Le Havre on my return from Ireland (from where de Valera's government had me deported on the orders of the Intelligence Service, which found me too revolutionary, that's to say too specifically Irish), I was, as I said, interned at Le Havre for having defended myself on the ship the *Washington* against an act of aggression which I suffered from a steward and a chief mechanic whom I accused of having been bribed by the police to make me disappear. That act of aggression having failed because the chief mechanic and the steward, who had cunningly entered my cabin with a monkey wrench, left again mad with fright, I was myself accused of hallucinating according to the usual procedure of all police forces, English or French, which consists of putting in a strait-jacket and throwing in a mental hospital all those whom they haven't killed or poisoned.[37]

When the boat docked at the port of Le Havre on 30 September, Artaud was immediately taken in the strait-jacket to the General Hospital. It was the start of an internment which lasted eight years and eight months.

4

Years of Incarceration

The asylum internment which Artaud underwent in the years from 1937 to 1946 has as much contradiction and productivity as the other phases of his life. But it was certainly the most deeply painful phase. The internment began with a period of self-preoccupation which Artaud broke only to berate his doctors and to demand external confirmation for the hallucinations he was experiencing. During the early part of Artaud's internment, at Rouen and Sainte-Anne, his behaviour gives the impression of great austerity and of a profound, self-sufficient calm. Although he spent his time in the company of the many different kinds of patients interned in the psychiatric hospitals of that time, he managed to enforce a degree of isolation and seclusion for himself. These first years of his internment, when Artaud was often kept in a cell, appear in some ways as a self-imposed recuperation and reconstitution after the mental shattering and the physical exhaustion of his sequence of journeys to Mexico, Brussels and Ireland. Artaud's attitude and bearing acquired a monastic quality. His condition was not a textbook psychosis; the many contradictory and wide-ranging medical diagnoses of his mental state indicate its flexibility and elusiveness. Within months of the total collapse which Artaud suffered after he was put in a strait-jacket on board the *Washington*, he was alert and lucid again. He became creatively preoccupied with the project of reformulating his identity, to the extent that he denied his identity as the interned Antonin Artaud to medical and social bodies, and even to his mother and friends.

This sense of a harsh but necessary convalescence soon evaporated. With the onset of the Second World War, his physical condition deteriorated seriously. Up to 1939 Artaud's principal grievances were against the drugs he was being administered, and the patients with whom he was kept. From the time of his transfer to the asylum of Ville-Évrard in February of that year, his position changed. He experienced a moment of exhilaration in August, when he finally formulated the new identity he had been working

towards since the summer of 1937. But the outbreak of the Second
World War in the following month, and the fall of Paris to the
Nazis in May 1940, led to starvation rations; Artaud became terribly emaciated. Ville-Évrard was one of the largest asylums in
France, which meant that Artaud's individual demands and hallucinations disappeared into an ocean of psychoses. The sharp hunger
and uncertainty of this time precipitated Artaud's return to writing
at Ville-Évrard; this new language was made up almost exclusively
of desperate pleas for food, heroin and liberation.

With his transfer to the asylum of Rodez in 1943, the parameters
of Artaud's internment were suddenly transformed. He found himself being fed regularly and well. He was treated by doctors who
were aware of his work, and wanted to have literary or theological
discussions with him. They also encouraged him to start writing
creatively again, and almost immediately they began to suggest the
possibility that Artaud's internment could be brought to an end
(although that would not happen for three years). Artaud was
allowed to go into the city streets and was able to meet local writers
and painters. But these doctors also administered fifty-one
unanaesthetized electroshock treatments which caused Artaud the
greatest torture of his life. During the same period he underwent a
religious crisis, which oscillated between a kind of gnostic Catholicism and an apocalyptic fury. At the beginning of 1945, Artaud
again began to write in a sustained way. Having started his internment with a silent interior dialogue that was indecipherable and
incommunicable to those around him, Artaud ended it with a
torrential creative output, which pulled him back into the outside
world and re-established his notoriety. He wrote more in the final
year of his internment at Rodez than in the entire seventeen years of
his literary, theatrical and film career in Paris. He also began to
draw, creating vivid images of his physical fragmentation. This
state of intense productivity never diminished. It crossed the border between Artaud's long asylum internment and his final period
of freedom.

At the General Hospital in Le Havre, Artaud lay on a bed in a
strait-jacket for seventeen days. From his cell, he could hear armies
fighting in the hospital grounds, trying to break through the walls
and release him. The armies were led by his friends; Breton was at
the head of one of the assaults, and was shot dead. Artaud's
hallucinations were all violent. He could hear the sounds of an

actress he had known in Paris, Colette Proust, being hacked to death with an axe in the cell next to his. For Artaud, these experiences were so authentic that he could never believe they had not happened. In 1946, when he met Breton again in Paris, Artaud reminded him of the incident, and of Breton's death. When Breton gently contradicted his memory, Artaud wept: the person he was talking to could not be the authentic André Breton who had fought for him at Le Havre. So, the true Breton had been replaced by a double.

Artaud was officially institutionalized on 16 October 1937, and transferred to the nearest psychiatric hospital, Quatre-Mares, at Sotteville-lès-Rouen in the southern suburbs of Rouen, halfway between Le Havre and Paris. His mother and friends were not informed. It was November before they decided to look for him. Paulhan wrote to the French Consul in Dublin on 18 November, and was told that Artaud had been deported on 29 September and shipped back to France. After trying the Le Havre hospitals, Artaud's mother discovered that her son was at Sotteville-lès-Rouen. She went to see him there, in a cell in the incurable patients' section; he refused to recognize her.

On 7 February 1938, *The Theatre and its Double* was finally published by Gallimard. Paulhan had excluded 'The Theatre of Séraphin' from the collection, despite Artaud's wish that it be included. Artaud was transferred to the Sainte-Anne asylum in Paris on 1 April 1938, at his mother's request. There he was shown the one and only review of his book, which appeared in the newspaper *Le Jour* on 27 April. It was a favourable review, but the author was anxious to mention her recent holiday in Finistère before dealing with Artaud's book.

At Sainte-Anne, Artaud was kept in the Henri-Rousselle clinic, where he had stayed before as a voluntary detoxification patient in 1932 and 1935. The doctors charged with supervising Artaud were named Nodet and Chapoulaud. After Artaud had been at Sainte-Anne for a fortnight, a provisional assessment of his condition was made: 'Literary pretensions, which are perhaps justified to the extent to which the delirium may serve as an inspiration. To be maintained.' Artaud must have had considerable contact with Jacques Lacan, the head of the clinic, since in a list compiled at Rodez he included him among the doctors who had treated him. Artaud would remember his time at Sainte-Anne as one of solitary confinement and poisoning: 'For 48 hours I was between life and death after swallowing a so-called powder against diarrhoea, which immediately gave me a terrible bloody dysentery, during which I fell on the edge of my bed.'[1] He refused to see his mother. His only other visitor was Roger Blin, who received the only known letters from Artaud of this period; one of the letters was spattered with blood and burned.[2] Blin was able to speak to Lacan about Artaud's condition through his contacts with Lacan's wife, the actress Sylvia Bataille (the former wife of Georges Bataille). He later described his visit to Sainte-Anne:

> I went to see Lacan one day, and I showed him the letters. He said that didn't interest him. I asked him if I could see Artaud for a moment, and he replied that Artaud didn't want to see anyone, which I believe was true . . . Lacan said to me: 'You can see him in the courtyard, there with the others.' And I saw Artaud, with a beard, although he had always been impeccably clean-shaven; he was leaning against a tree. Around him, the others were playing football. I tried to attract his attention, without success, but probably he wouldn't have wanted to talk to me.[3]

After eleven months at Sainte-Anne, Artaud was transferred to the larger asylum of Ville-Évrard, in the eastern suburbs of Paris, on 27 February 1939. At Sainte-Anne, the only diagnosis that had been made as to his condition was that he was chronically and incurably insane. For the journey to Ville-Évrard, Artaud was again put in a strait-jacket. He would complain many times that one of the male nurses accompanying him had kicked him in the testicles. At Ville-Évrard, Artaud was again kept in a cell, and he was constantly moved from ward to ward during his stay: 'I passed three abominable years at Ville-Évrard, transferred without motive or reason from the maniacs' ward (the 6th) to the epileptics' ward (the 4th), from the epileptics' ward to the cripples' ward (the 2nd), and from the cripples' ward to the undesirables' ward (the 10th).'[4] His hair was cropped very close to his head, and he was given an asylum inmate's uniform to wear. The doctors at Ville-Évrard who treated him were named Chanès and Menuau; Artaud detested them. Two young house-doctors were training at Ville-Évrard, Michel Lubtchansky and Léon Fouks, and Artaud had more friendly relations with these men. Lubtchansky was the only one of the doctors from Artaud's previous asylums who wrote to him at Rodez to see how he was getting on. At Ville-Évrard he was diagnosed as exhibiting a syndrome of delirium, of the paranoid type, and as being incurable. (Lacan had written his doctoral thesis on paranoid psychosis, but no such diagnosis was made at Sainte-Anne.) Although Artaud was kept at Ville-Évrard for almost four years, until January 1943, it appears that no attempt was made to apply any particular treatment; to a large extent, he was left to himself as a patient who calmly complied with orders. In July 1942, Artaud's mother asked his doctors whether the new, and increasingly used therapy of electroshock might be applied on her son; at this time, electroshock was widely seen as an innovative way of inducing apparently miraculous results. Artaud's doctors ignored the suggestion, on the grounds that the treatment would not be beneficial.

Soon after arriving at Ville-Évrard, Artaud stopped refusing to see his mother. He also accepted visits from his sister, Marie-Ange, who brought her two children to see him. In the period leading up to the fall of Paris in May 1940, Artaud was able to see a number of friends who made the journey out from Paris to visit him. They included Roger Blin, Sonia Mossé, Anne Manson, Pierre Souvtchinsky, and Génica Athanasiou – Artaud was so eager to see her that he even invited her to bring her lover Jean Grémillon along. He often demanded heroin – which he believed would help him to resist the malicious forces of magic holding him captive – especially from Génica Athanasiou and Roger Blin, whose father was a doctor. In June 1941, he begged Anie Besnard to come and visit him:

> My beloved Angel
> it's now eight months that I've been waiting for you here
> day after day hour after hour and by moments
> second after second.[5]

He told her that she must leave Paris, which had become 'a centre of demoniac infection *where you must not set foot again*'.[6] He also sent her a great list of different foods which he wanted her to bring to the asylum, in addition to heroin. A week later, on 3 July, Anie Besnard visited Artaud in the company of René Thomas, in whose studio Artaud had stayed before his journey to Ireland. Anie Besnard considered that Artaud looked like a monk, with his shorn hair, austere clothes, and his isolation from the other inmates. Artaud was not happy with the visit: Anie Besnard had not come to release him from the asylum, as he had demanded, and so she must be a demon who had seized his friend's body. On the same day, he wrote to her:

> This is to say that neither
> you nor René Thomas
> can come back here
> neither next Thursday
> nor ever because those who
> carried their names in 1937
> and who sheltered Antonin
> Artaud are dead . . .[7]

In 1945 at Rodez, Artaud would make the same demands upon Anie Besnard, and impose the same rejection. Towards the end of his time at Ville-Évrard, the circumstances of the war made it difficult for Artaud's friends to get there, and only his mother made regular visits.

In August 1939, Artaud decided to put an end to the existence of Antonin Artaud, the forty-two-year-old writer from a bourgeois family who had suffered such humiliation from the Parisian literary milieu, and who was now being imprisoned, deprived of opium and heroin, in an insane asylum. Rather than committing suicide, Artaud executed the transformation of identity which had been seething in him since the time of *The New Revelations of Being*. The new identity Artaud chose was that of Antonin Nalpas. Nalpas was his mother's maiden name, and he had a distant cousin named Antonin Nalpas. By this act of overturning his parents' marriage (and, therefore, his birth within it), Artaud began a huge operation of genealogical inversion and familial reformulation, which eventually led to the creation of his new family of 'daughters of the heart to be born' at Rodez. The operation was completed, back in Paris, with Artaud's final assertions of absolute self-responsibility and self-generation for his own identity, body, birth and death. Antonin Nalpas was conceived at Ville-Évrard as a new, pure, virginal and miraculous body. Although Artaud signed his letters with just 'Antonin' during the subsequent two years, by December 1941 he was signing them 'Antonin Nalpas'; he refused any other identity. He would write to Dr Ferdière at Rodez in 1943:

> Antonin Artaud died from sorrow and pain at Ville-Évrard in the month of August 1939 and his corpse left Ville-Évrard during the course of a white night, like those which Dostoyevsky speaks of, which took up the space of several days . . .
> I succeeded him and added myself to him soul for soul and body for body in a body which formed itself in his bed, concretely and in reality, but by magic, in the place of his body . . .
> My own name, Dr Ferdière, is Antonin Nalpas . . .[8]

In addition to this internal work of self-recreation, Artaud wrote many letters during the early part of his stay at Ville-Évrard, especially during the first three months. In a letter of 4 March 1939, only a week after his arrival, Artaud complained to the Parisian bookshop owner Adrienne Monnier about the violence of his transfer from Sainte-Anne. He developed a complex historical narrative about malicious doubles who invaded the bodies of writers and musicians, to steal their work. He asserted that he was himself a victim of this; his writings on the Tarahumaras were the fourth project to be stolen. And he concluded that his work would have to be started all over again. The letter possessed a furious lucidity, despite its sudden shifts in scope and attitude. Adrienne Monnier had never met Artaud, but she published his letter in April 1939 in her magazine *La Gazette des Amis du Livre*, thereby angering Paulhan, who felt that Artaud's internment should be treated with more discretion.

Two months after writing the letter to Adrienne Monnier, Artaud produced a new set of the 'spells' which he had sent as threats and protections from Dublin in September 1937. (The letter from Sainte-Anne which Roger Blin described as being blood-spattered and burned may also have been a 'spell'.) These new 'spells' had a much more intricate design, and Artaud's doctors put different coloured inks at his disposal. The 'spells' were meticulously constructed, using drawings of signs and layers of colour. A violent element of chance was then put to work; Artaud inflicted cigarette burns upon the paper of the 'spell', which served as an intermediary for the body of the person who was under attack. The text of the 'spell' was often burned almost to the point of obliteration. Artaud gave one 'spell' to the house-doctor Léon Fouks as a protection, and Dr Lubtchansky kept a 'spell' which Artaud had produced as a warning to an occultist named Grillot de Givry, who had died in 1929. Artaud believed that Grillot de Givry was persecuting him with magic, and the 'spell' contained a declaration of its own power:

> Its efficacy of action
> is immediate and
> *and eternal*.
> And it *breaks* every
> *bewitchment*.[9]

Blin received a 'spell' which contained a ferocious warning to the people whom Artaud believed were preventing him from receiving

heroin. Sonia Mossé was sent 'a Force of Death'.[10] The final 'spell'
was addressed to Adolf Hitler, probably at the outbreak of the
Second World War on 3 September 1939. Its content oscillated
between cordial advice and threatening invective:

> P.S. Of course, dear Sir
> this is hardly an invita-
> tion! it's above all a
> warning.[11]

After the name Antonin Nalpas had entered Artaud's letters in
December 1941, he went through a period of hardly writing at all.
However, he continued to make demands for food parcels from his
mother (whom he addressed by her first name). On 23 March 1942
he wrote:

> And I repeat to you, my dearest Euphrasie, it is absolutely false
> that provisions are scarce in Paris. All the other *inmates* receive an
> abundance of provisions in the form of butter, cheese, dates, real
> spice-bread, figs, apples, pears, REAL jams, sugar, chocolate, ban-
> anas. Your maid and your supplier have, moreover, lied to you in
> claiming that chocolate, bananas, walnuts and hazelnuts are reserved
> for children. I know all about this: there is no law, no regulation, not
> even any police recommendations in that direction, for the good
> reason that all the children of France are eating in my own belly.[12]

The onset of the war – which Artaud viewed with detachment as
being apocalyptic – had brought severe food shortages to the
asylum, and the danger of eventual deportation to the Nazi concentration camps for 'incurable' patients like Artaud. The starvation
rations (cabbage soup) continued relentlessly, and Artaud began to
suffer from malnutrition; by the spring of 1942, his weight had
dropped to fifty-two kilogrammes. He believed that his survival was
due principally to his physical resilience: 'If I am still alive, Euphrasie, it is because of an abnormally resistant constitution . . . in
reality, Euphrasie, I am no more than a living corpse who sees
himself surviving and I live here with the anguishes of death.'[13]

In September 1942, Artaud's mother approached Robert Desnos
to see if he could find a solution to Artaud's precarious situation.
Desnos had not been to see Artaud at Ville-Évrard but he responded quickly to the appeal. He had a friend named Gaston Ferdière,
a Surrealist poet with anarchic tendencies, who was then head
psychiatrist at the mental hospital of Rodez, in the south-west of

France. At this time, Gaston Ferdière was thirty-five years old. (Ferdière continued to practise psychiatry until well into his eighties at a private clinic in Aubervilliers, in the northern suburbs of Paris, where he specialized in nervous disorders; he was still writing Surrealist poetry that was 'too obscene to be published'.)[14] Rodez was in the zone of France that was officially unoccupied by the German army. Although a considerable military presence was visible there, life for the inhabitants was much more stable than in Paris. Desnos knew that Artaud would be better cared-for and fed at Rodez than at Ville-Évrard. He contacted Ferdière, who immediately agreed to accept Artaud as a patient at his hospital. He even suggested that he could pick up Artaud personally, since he would be in Paris over Christmas 1942. But administrative problems arose, and this plan became impossible. It was forbidden to transfer a patient from the Occupied Zone to the Unoccupied Zone. Ferdière overcame this. He had previously run an asylum at Chezal-Benoît, close to the border between the two zones. He used his remaining influence there to arrange for Artaud to be transferred initially to Chezal-Benoît, before being imperceptibly transferred again to Rodez. Desnos went to visit Artaud at Ville-Évrard on the day before his transfer to Chezal-Benoît, and was shocked by Artaud's physical state. Artaud was terrified that by leaving Ville-Évrard for yet another asylum, he would become defenceless against the magical forces which harassed him. He was transferred from Ville-Évrard on 22 January 1943, after nearly four years, accompanied by two nurses. At Chezal-Benoît, where Artaud remained for nineteen days, he was examined and diagnosed as suffering from paranoid psychosis and a delirium that was 'very active but badly systematized'. It was noted that he spoke of Antonin Artaud as though he were a stranger. Artaud still complained of being desperately hungry at Chezal-Benoît: 'I am bedridden and dying from the lack of sugar, *hazelnuts*, walnuts, dates, figs and chocolate.'[15] Having heard about Gaston Ferdière from Desnos, Artaud claimed that he had already met Ferdière in 1935 at Desnos's apartment. He was already anticipating that Ferdière would be his liberator. During the transfer from Chezal-Benoît to Rodez on 10 February 1943, Artaud lost the sword he had received in 1936 at the voodoo ceremony in Cuba, and which he had kept with him ever since.

On Artaud's arrival at Rodez, Ferdière took a photograph of him in his Ville-Évrard uniform and with his shorn hair. At Rodez,

Artaud wore old second-hand suits and grew his hair long. Ferdière's initial diagnosis was that Artaud was suffering from 'a chronic and extremely intense delirium characterized by persecution . . . Transformation of the personality, of his official identity. His personality is double, etc . . .; ideas of persecution with periods of marked violent reactions.' Artaud was treated kindly. Ferdière invited him to dinner with his wife, and gave him all the food he wanted; Artaud quickly regained weight. In addition to food, he demanded a daily bath and a toothbrush for his eight remaining teeth. (His other teeth had apparently been lost at the previous asylums, through the wretched diet.) He wrote to Paulhan demanding royalties for a huge edition of *The Theatre and its Double* which he believed had appeared in November 1937, to great acclaim. This imaginary edition had sold one hundred thousand copies; the actual edition of the book published in February 1938 had consisted of only four hundred copies.

Artaud's demands increased. In June 1943, he asked Ferdière for opium, on the grounds that it would cure the bout of dysentery he was suffering from; Ferdière refused. Artaud was spending a great deal of his time humming, gesturing and spitting to defend himself against the demonic figures he could see. He had done this at Ville-Évrard, where it was ignored in the more general cacophony. Artaud would justify his activity by relating it to the ideas about breathing and gesture he had explored in his text 'An Affective Athleticism'. He told Ferdière that 'if it is a sickness for me to engage in this, then Antonin Artaud has always been sick because all his theatre direction consisted of nothing other than that'.[16] Ferdière detested Artaud's noises and gestures; he wanted Artaud to return to sustained literary writing. His position was that Artaud was 'violently anti-social, dangerous for public order and people's security'.[17] He believed that Artaud could never be cured, but that he might be returned to a more creative and socially useful life. For all these reasons, Ferdière took the decision in June 1943 to give Artaud a series of electroshock treatments.

Electroshock treatment was still in its infancy; its aura of innovation attracted Ferdière. The treatment had been developed from initial research in 1934 by Laszlo Meduna on the links between schizophrenia and epilepsy. In 1938, the Italian doctor Ugo Cerletti went to the Rome abattoir and watched the pigs being slaughtered: an electric shock to the skull subdued them and made it less troublesome for them to be killed. Cerletti applied the principle directly to his patients' brains and discovered that the shock reduced their symptoms and made them more docile. Cerletti also experimented with injecting the spinal fluid of electroshocked pigs into his patients, but without success. Electroshock treatment is now generally discredited; it is still used in some countries to treat cases of extreme depression, and is applied with anaesthetic. But in 1943 it was becoming a popular form of treatment for a wide range of mental disorders; many psychiatrists stubbornly believed that the temporary and clinically ungaugeable effects of the dangerous treatment were not due solely to the patient's stunned terror at the prospect of its next application. The prominent writer on electroshock treatment, Max Fink, has commented: 'The resolution of the men who introduced convulsive therapy is astonishing.'[18] The treatment consisted of attaching electrodes to the patient's temples and then sending a short burst of electrical current through the brain, without anaesthetic. The patient was tied down to avoid the limbs fracturing during the convulsions that followed. A spatula was placed in the patient's mouth to prevent the teeth breaking against each other or the tongue being bitten through. A coma of fifteen to thirty minutes followed the convulsions, after which the patient awoke with a memory loss which often provoked a great sense of anguish. A course of thirty electroshocks was common, although courses extending into the hundreds – 'annihilation therapy', as it was called in the United States – were recorded. Between June 1943 and December 1944, Artaud had fifty-one electroshocks.

Ferdière, who always maintained that the therapy was painless, did not administer the treatment to Artaud himself. It was executed by his assistant, a young and devout Roman Catholic named Jacques Latrémolière, with whom Artaud had many theological discussions. (According to Gaston Ferdière, Latrémolière later became a deeply disturbed man, obsessed with mystical concerns.)[19] In his doctoral thesis of 1944, *Incidents and Accidents observed in the course of 1,200 Electroshocks*, Latrémolière described Artaud's treatment:

> A., 46 years old, former drug addict, suffering from chronic hallucinatory psychosis, with luxuriant, polymorphous, delirious ideas (doubling of the personality, bizarre metaphysical system . . .).
> The patient had gained five kilogrammes in weight when the treatment began on 20 June. From the second session on, he spoke of vague back pains, which became violent when he awoke from the

third crisis: bilateral, constrictive, increased by the slightest movement, and by coughing, the pains forced him to walk in a bent-over
position, with the thorax leaning out to the front.

After this third electroshock, Artaud had to spend two months in
bed convalescing, and receiving injections of histamine. One of his
vertebrae had been fractured. At his Vieux-Colombier lecture of
January 1947, Artaud described a further incident. He said that one
of his subsequent electroshock comas lasted ninety minutes instead
of the usual fifteen to thirty, and Ferdière had already ordered that
his body be dispatched to the mortuary when he suddenly regained
consciousness. Once he had been released from Rodez, Artaud's
denunciations of his electroshock treatments had an immense ferocity. (In old age, Ferdière was renowned for weeping at Parisian
literary gatherings when the subject was brought up of Artaud's
great bitterness towards him.) In 1943, after the first electroshocks,
Artaud's appeals to Ferdière were intensely pitiful:

> My very dear friend,
> I have a great service and a great favour to ask of you. This is to
> cut short the application of electroshocks on me, which my body
> obviously cannot stand and which are certainly the predominant,
> revealing cause of my present vertebral displacement. As I told you
> this morning, my belief in demons has disappeared and I am sure it
> will not return, but what remains is this unbearable sensation of
> shattering in the back, which I believe can only be attributed to this
> violent electrical treatment that has had an undeniable effect, but
> which it would certainly be undesirable to prolong for any more time
> upon me, in order not to risk more dangerous accidents![20]

But when Artaud's back healed, the treatments started again. Latrémolière wrote in his thesis:

> The intensity of the delirium persisted; the good effects of the first
> three sessions, which had very clearly diminished the bizarre and
> theatrical reactions of the subject in the face of his hallucinations,
> encouraged us to resume a new series of 12 electroshocks from 25
> October to 22 November 1943.
> No back pain arose that would have indicated an aggravation of
> the process of collapse, and the patient can now lead a normal life in
> the asylum, and devote himself to intellectual works which he would
> have been incapable of before the shocks.

Nevertheless, thirty-six further electroshocks would be given to
Artaud in the course of the following year.

At the end of Artaud's first summer at Rodez, Ferdière tried another therapy. He gave Artaud written translations to undertake, and requested that he should begin writing sustained texts instead of only letters. Ferdière presented the therapy as a personal service which Artaud could do for him; he was planning to edit a series of books at Rodez, and said that he needed Artaud's help. Ferdière enlisted the aid of a young Surrealist painter from Marseilles, Frédéric Delanglade – who had escaped from a prisoner-of-war camp and was hiding from the Germans in Rodez – to encourage Artaud to start work. The first project was a number of translations from the works of Lewis Carroll (a favourite of Ferdière), in particular the chapter from *Through the Looking Glass* in which Alice meets Humpty-Dumpty. Although this work must have appeared to Artaud as a recapitulation of the translations he had done for financial reasons in 1930 and 1932, he began the work with some enthusiasm. This soon dispersed, and he developed a personal animosity towards Lewis Carroll. Nevertheless, the translation provided an opportunity to engage with the linguistic games and manipulations of Humpty-Dumpty. (He would return to his translation from *Through the Looking Glass* in 1947 and revise it, declaring that the chapter now belonged to him, rather than to Lewis Carroll; he subtitled his reworked translation *Anti-Grammatical Attempt on Lewis Carroll and Against Him*.) Since Artaud knew very little English, he collaborated with the asylum chaplain on literal transcriptions, and then used them to make free adaptations of the texts. Other translations followed, of poems by Edgar Allan Poe, Robert Southwell and John Keats.

In October 1943, Artaud wrote a long poetic text entitled *KAB-HAR ENIS – KATHAR ESTI*, partly made up from a language he was in the process of inventing. He attempted to send the text to Paulhan, but all his mail was inspected at Rodez and the poem never reached Paulhan; Jacques Latrémolière kept it. Artaud also wrote a critical account of a story he had read by Marcel Béalu, 'The Open Mouth', which Ferdière retained. In December 1943, Artaud received the first proposal to publish his writings since he had been interned in 1937. Through the intermediary of the writer Henri Parisot, a young poet and occultist named Robert-J. Godet requested permission to reprint as a booklet the text 'On a Journey to the Land of the Tarahumaras', which had been published in *La Nouvelle Revue Française* in 1937. Godet also wanted to know if Artaud had any unpublished material about his journey to Mexico.

Artaud immediately wrote a new text on the Tarahumaras which he showed to Ferdière, who kept it. (In 1947, after Artaud had left Rodez, the publisher Marc Barbezat – already renowned as the first publisher of Jean Genet's fiction – took up the project for a book of Artaud's writings on the Tarahumaras, and succeeded in persuading Ferdière to send him a copy of this text.) In addition to the new writing on his journey to Mexico, Artaud was also considering a book about his journey to Ireland, which he now believed was the more crucial of his two great journeys. Ferdière began to encourage Artaud to work on images as well as writings. In mid-October 1943, Artaud took his first photograph since the photo-montages he had worked on for the Alfred Jarry Theatre in 1930. The photograph was intended to illustrate a nursery rhyme Ferdière was interested in, and showed a cabbage on a stick in the asylum gardens.

In the face of the electroshocks and Ferdière's incessant urging that Artaud resume his identity as a writer, the identity of Antonin Nalpas, which Artaud had sustained for four years, could no longer hold out. Much to Ferdière's satisfaction, he abandoned it in September 1943 after a 'terrible upheaval'. Artaud could then state to Ferdière: 'I am called Antonin Artaud, because I am the son of Antoine Artaud and of Euphrasie Artaud, who is still alive although my father died in Marseilles in September 1924.'[21] But this period, when 'Antonin Artaud' grudgingly re-emerged, was probably that of the deepest fluctuation and loss of identity in Artaud's life. His short-lived religious convictions arose from this shattering of the self. Often during 1943 and 1944, Artaud adopted a pious Catholicism and went to pray in the cathedral at Rodez. But his mystical feelings were in a state of great flux, so that he would, on alternate days, pray with and insult the asylum chaplain. At times, he counterbalanced the fearful uncertainty of his present situation by extending his piety back into the past, to produce a sense of stability and continuity: 'If from Dublin to here at Rodez I have not practised religion, it is because there was no Church at Sotteville-lès-Rouen, Sainte-Anne, or Ville-Évrard.'[22] At other times, his religious feelings would be his own imaginative creation, transformed until they sympathetically served the immediate needs of his position: 'God, by nature, is a bizarre being who has only ever loved rebels and madmen.'[23] This continual oscillation lasted until 1 April 1945, when Artaud definitively rejected all religions: 'I have thrown the communion, the eucharist, god and his christ out of the window and have decided to be myself . . .'[24]

The return of his original identity had further repercussions, particularly in connection with his concept of society. Struggling to erase all traits which could be construed by Ferdière as anti-social, and therefore the justification for more electroshocks, Artaud suddenly became deeply attached to his family and to the French nation. In October 1943, he wrote to Paulhan and declared: 'You know I have always been a royalist and a patriot.'[25] He demanded that Paulhan should pulp all his books, with the exceptions of the letters to Rivière, *The Theatre and its Double* and *The New Revelations of Being*. Around the same period, he was also writing letters – which Ferdière kept – to the President of the Nazi-controlled French Government, Pierre Laval. Laval had attended a performance of *The Cenci* in 1935, and Artaud considered him to be a friend. (Laval was shot as a traitor at the end of the war, for collaborating with the Germans.) Artaud appealed to Laval to help free him from the asylum. With absolute conviction, he denied that he was mad: 'And really, I do not believe that I have ever been affected by the least shadow of mental disturbance.'[26] He complained about the loss of his cane in Ireland, and expressed his contempt for the English people – whose police he regarded as responsible for his arrest in Dublin – and for their military forces, with the exception of the Royal Air Force (which he believed was composed mainly of Scotsmen). Since Artaud perceived a parallel between the devastation which Hitler was inflicting on the world and the apocalyptic prophecies of *The New Revelations of Being*, he now dedicated a copy of his book to Hitler. Like Jean Genet and Louis-Ferdinand Céline, Artaud had his own individual and contradictory reasons for favouring a force that had overpowered French society.

At the beginning of 1944, Ferdière tried another new treatment on Artaud, art therapy. Although the painter Frédéric Delanglade had departed for Paris by this time, he had left behind some charcoal sticks and crayons. Delanglade had also painted a portrait of Artaud in the studio he had set up in the asylum. In February 1944, Artaud executed a number of charcoal drawings on small sheets of paper, showing signs and faces. One drawing was of the sword Artaud had received in Cuba and recently lost. Ferdière set much importance by this therapy, and later styled himself as one of the great pioneering figures of Art Psychotherapy. Ferdière's approach was that the patient's image should serve largely as a diagnostic indicator. (This runs in direct contradiction to the

concept of art therapy developed in the 1980s by Dr Leo Navratil at
the Klosterneuberg mental hospital near Vienna. Navratil arranged
for the construction of a special pavilion in the asylum grounds for
patients who wanted to live there and draw; the artists are free to
draw whatever they desire without clinical evaluation. Artists working in such conditions, such as August Walla and Johann Hauser,
have produced some of this century's most compelling images of
the human body.) Ferdière disliked Artaud's drawings and considered them 'of no interest whatsoever'.[27] After the first few
drawings of February 1944 undertaken at Ferdière's instigation,
Artaud abandoned drawing for a year. When he began again, the
drawings emerged from his own sense of creative necessity.

From 23 May to 10 June 1944, Artaud received twelve electroshocks; in August 1944, another twelve; and in December 1944,
another twelve. By this period, he had long since started the writings which Ferdière had requested of him, and these new electroshocks revived Artaud's terror of the memory loss which they
caused, and exacerbated his back pain. His remaining teeth fell out.
The electroshocks appeared to him as a multitude of little deaths –
not the 'petite mort' of orgasm of which Georges Bataille wrote, nor
the sensation of euphoria at the onset of an epileptic fit, but a period
of absolutely cold, senseless loss, repeated without a determinable
end. There have been numerous reports of psychiatrists becoming
addicted to the electroshocks which they gave to their patients. The
December 1944 electroshocks were Artaud's last. On several
occasions after his release from Rodez, Artaud asserted that he had
had to threaten violence against Ferdière to bring the electroshocks
to a close. At his Vieux-Colombier lecture in January 1947, Artaud
said: 'I do not think that I can let myself be taken for a coward, and
on a certain day of December 1944 I threatened to jump on top of
Dr Ferdière and strangle him if he did not immediately forget the
idea of the new series of electroshocks which he wanted to apply to
me.'[28] However, Ferdière was still prepared to intimidate Artaud
with the prospect of further electroshocks whenever Artaud tried to
convince him of the authenticity of his hallucinations, or practised
his humming techniques in the asylum grounds. It was also in 1944
that Artaud suffered the first of a number of severe intestinal
haemorrhages. He believed that they were the result of the starvation he had suffered at Ville-Évrard, but they may well have been a
first indication of the cancer which would remain undiagnosed until
February 1948.

It was in January 1945 that Artaud's creative capacities came back to him with great strength, and he never stopped working from then until his death three years later. The final work threw out images and writings with ferocious force. For Ferdière, this return to work was the result of the treatments he had applied, including the electroshocks – without these treatments, the final phase of Artaud's work would simply not exist.[29] This is extremely unlikely. Artaud had declared in the 1930s that he could only work through the absence of opium; now, he started to work from the time when the electroshocks were absent from his life. The war was coming to a close, and Paris had been liberated from the German Occupation on 23 August 1944. Artaud was slowly able to re-establish contact with his friends there. He also formed a strong friendship with a young doctor who came to work at Rodez in February 1945, Jean Dequeker. Dequeker gave Artaud great encouragement, and supported his violent creative resurgence. He understood Artaud's need to battle physically against the forces he believed were oppressing him. In opposition to Ferdière, Dequeker approved of the humming and chanting exercises which Artaud was developing to fortify his new language and images. Dequeker had to leave Rodez temporarily in the spring of 1945 to work at a hospital for repatriated prisoners-of-war at Mulhouse, in eastern France, and he and Artaud continued their dialogue by letter. He then returned to Rodez, and was still there when Artaud was released in May 1946. According to Ferdière, Dequeker suffered from severe depression in later years and was himself confined, in a nursing home.[30]

Artaud began his new work in January 1945 with a series of drawings. The writings would follow on from the drawings, as though hauled back into existence by the power of Artaud's visual imagery. Working on large sheets of paper and still using the pencils, coloured chalks and children's crayola crayons that Delanglade had left at Rodez, Artaud began a visual exploration of his physical and mental condition during the years of incarceration. Over a period of seventeen months, the drawings built from impressions of shattered powerlessness to controlled and intricate evocations of physical fragmentation and reconstitution. Artaud drew fields of human dissection and torture, filled with splinters and spikes, cancers and broken, bleeding bodies. In these drawings, he split and broke the human body, grinding it with his crayons into the surface of the paper, as a substance to be collapsed and then reformulated from zero. The body's inner space was extracted, spat out, with great tension and movement, into the exterior world. Around the principal figures in the drawings, other forms and objects fell blindly through space. In drawings with such titles as *The being and its foetuses* and *Never real and always true*, Artaud's figures appeared acutely disjointed, manipulated with precision to occupy a space of dismemberment. Pieces of metal, insects, tiny girls' faces, penises, internal organs, all spilled out in a painful dispersal across the furrowed surface of the paper. Old machinery and propellors intersected with swollen human shapes and lacerated faces.

The drawings from Rodez project Artaud's deep sense of his disrupted body and its disintegrated language. This sense was magnified by his recent experiences of electroshock. Short texts were introduced around the edges of his drawings. His language was put back together again as an amalgamation of image and text, in the same period that he was also attempting to put his body and consciousness back together again. As the drawings developed, Artaud often surrounded and penetrated them with phrases from the invented language which he continued to elaborate up until his death, inserting it as an enraged incantation into his work. The phrases served as protections for his newly resuscitated work, which he felt was vulnerable to malicious suppression and failure. The Rodez drawings carry the corporeal force which would also be in Artaud's recorded screams of 1948. The images emerged on the paper from a process of internal incision and interrogation. They manifest an instinctual articulation of the body in disunity, adrift in an oceanic space of abject negativity and deep desire. Towards the end of Artaud's internment, his drawings became the raw material for the probing of fears – about the loss of his right to determine his identity, about the threats to his body – which he would rework in many different ways until the end of his life. In the last of the series of drawings from Rodez, Artaud turned to his own face as the most sensitive site for expressing his fear of attack and his determination to counterattack. He drew his first self-portrait for twenty years. Dequeker watched Artaud's work on this image, and later described what he saw:

> I was present for several days at the drilling of such an image, at the savage hammerings of a form which was not his own. On a large sheet of white paper, he had drawn the abstract contours of a face, and within this barely sketched material – where he had planted the

black marks of future apparitions – and without a reflecting mirror, I
saw him create his double, as though in a crucible, at the cost of an
unspeakable torture and cruelty. He worked with rage, shattering
pencil after pencil, suffering the internal throes of his own exorcism.
At the heart of the most inflamed screams and poems which had ever
emerged from his tortured spleen, he struck and cursed a nation of
stubborn worms – then suddenly, he seized reality, and his face
appeared. This was the terrible lucidity of the creation of Antonin
Artaud by himself – the terrible mask of all the enslaved horizons –
launched as an act of defiance against the poor means and the
mediocre techniques of painters of reality. Through the creative rage
with which he exploded the bolts of reality and all the latches of the
surreal, I saw him blindly dig out the eyes of his image.[31]

In February 1945, the month after his drawings began to emerge,
Artaud set to work writing short fragments in school exercise-
books. He wrote every day, and the number of fragments soon
accumulated. Through the sheer relentlessness and driving obsess-
iveness of this work, he taught himself how to write again with all
the force and fluency he had possessed before his internment.
Occasionally these fragments would lead to more developed texts,
such as 'Surrealism and the End of the Christian Era' from October
1945. This text (part of which was lost, and another part stolen)
recalls his open letters from the time of the collaboration with the
Surrealists, in 1925. In 'Surrealism and the End of the Christian
Era', Artaud writes of his realization, at the age of eight, that his
identity was to be threatened by malicious powers, illness and
cacophony all through his life. His attitude remained as independent as ever: 'I have never studied anything, but lived everything,
and that has taught me something.'[32] He also wrote a number of
commentaries on his drawings. They were mostly requested as
'explanatory' texts by Ferdière and Latrémolière, but Artaud
always ensured that they veered wildly from such a function. He
was also contemplating a reworking of his ideas on the theatre: 'I
am preparing another book on the Theatre, but from a much larger
and more general point of view than *The Theatre and its Double* – it
will, I believe, interest an extensive public.'[33] But it was principally
the exercise-book fragments which consumed Artaud and provoked
his imagination throughout 1945 and the first months of 1946. He
worked over old concerns, such as peyote and the Irish cane, and
drew up enormous lists of food, as he had at Ville-Évrard. More
vitally, an endless reconstruction took place of his relationship with

his friends and enemies in Paris, his family, and also with public figures he had never actually met, such as Stalin, de Gaulle, Churchill, and Freud. Jean Genet wrote that Artaud struggled, during his internment, to discover what would lead him 'to glory . . . into the light'.[34] Artaud searched for a new, living and liberated body from the material of these multiple reformulations and dialogues, and finally found it towards the end of 1945 with the creation of his 'daughters of the heart to be born'.

These 'daughters' were a highly charged, sexually imbued and manipulable group. Artaud usually imagined six daughters for himself, but he could, when necessary, incorporate other women into the existing children. The daughters combined purely imaginative elements with presences from Artaud's past life. Both of his grandmothers became daughters, as did Cécile Schramme, Yvonne Allendy and Anie Besnard. The daughters fought for him, and suffered terrible tortures in their efforts to reach him at Rodez and free him. Artaud was always certain of their imminent arrival. He wrote to Anie Besnard on 29 October 1945: 'I am awaiting you as arranged, together with your sister Catherine, for whom I no longer have an address, and Cécile, Yvonne and Neneka. You have suffered far too much for anything to stop you and hold you back this time . . .'[35] Around March 1946, he made a drawing entitled *The theatre of cruelty*, which shows four of the daughters in coffins, placed across one another at tangents. Their bodies are scarred and mummified, and they are guarded by an immense, distorted, bird-like creature, but their eyes are open and alert. After his release from Rodez, Artaud wrote to Gilbert Lély, the biographer of the Marquis de Sade, describing the origin of his daughters:

> I thought a lot about love at the asylum of Rodez, and it was there that I dreamed about some daughters of my soul, who loved me like daughters, and not as lovers – me, their pre-pubescent, lustful, salacious, erotic and incestuous father;
> and chaste also, so chaste that it makes him dangerous.[36]

The effusively imaginative creation of Artaud's daughters of the heart gave him a great sense of anticipation and hope, which helped to pull him through his last year at Rodez. It also provided him with allies for his struggle, a new family, and a new sexuality.

Artaud dispassionately watched the war coming to an end during the spring of 1945; he still considered it to be a manifestation of the apocalypse, but nevertheless of no great concern to him. The

Germans surrendered in May, and the war in Europe was over. Robert Desnos died of typhoid fever on 8 June in the newly liberated concentration camp of Theresienstadt in Czechoslovakia. He had been arrested in Paris by the Gestapo for his Resistance work in February 1944, a year after he had helped Artaud to reach Rodez. As Artaud had been moved from one asylum to another, so Desnos had passed through the concentration camps of Auschwitz, Buchenwald, Flossenburg and Flora. Artaud heard of his death in August, and wrote a sorrowful letter to Desnos's widow Youki, inviting her to join with the women who were coming to Rodez to liberate him. Some months later, Artaud heard that his friend Sonia Mossé had died in the gas chamber of a concentration camp.

Around 10 September 1945, Artaud had his first visitors at Rodez, the painter Jean Dubuffet and his wife. (Raymond Queneau had wanted to visit Artaud at the end of 1943, but Ferdière had told him that Artaud was still too ill.) Artaud showed Dubuffet his recent drawings, and the visit made him impatient to return to a life in Paris. Ferdière was now seriously considering his release, but Artaud was aware that Ferdière would require substantial guarantees that Artaud's future would be financially secure. After Dubuffet had returned to Paris, Artaud elaborated the existence of a bank account containing a huge sum in gold bars, which he claimed to have deposited in 1918. Since Dubuffet was a man with much financial expertise, Artaud wrote to the Bank of France instructing them to hand over the contents of the account to Dubuffet, to administer on his behalf. But the Bank of France wrote back to say that they knew nothing of Artaud's account. He had also set Dubuffet to work locating his real and imaginary 'daughter of the heart' in Paris.

On the night of 2 December, Artaud's publisher Robert Denoël was shot dead in the street while changing a wheel on his car. It is probable that he was assassinated for political reasons (as a reputed Nazi collaborator, and as the publisher of Céline's anti-Semitic books), but the shooting remained a mystery; he may have been attacked by a thief, or simply shot at random by one of the gangs roaming Paris at the time. Artaud heard of Denoël's death on 6 December, and soon incorporated it into his conviction that all his friends were being murdered in order to leave him in a state of isolation. But he also had a financial grudge against Denoël: 'Don't forget that Denoël, who has since been assassinated, had me transferred to Rodez in order not to have to pay me my royalties on a new edition of *The New Revelations of Being* and of *Heliogabalus* (at least 50 to 80,000 *pre-war* francs).'[37]

Between September and December 1945, Artaud wrote a series of inflammatory and caustic letters to Henri Parisot, who re-issued Artaud's text *On a Journey to the Land of the Tarahumaras* in November 1945. In these letters, Artaud reformulated the history of his life as an endless succession of torturings, detentions and assassination attempts, starting with the story of the knife-wound inflicted by the Marseilles pimp in 1915. Artaud proudly declared that he had violently returned every assault and bewitchment he received. Parisot was the perfect recipient for the letters, since he always expressed tentative reservations about what Artaud was telling him, thereby impelling Artaud into a state of still greater inventiveness and fury. Parisot also asked Artaud to write in ink rather than pencil, since he was short-sighted; Artaud angrily retorted that he could not use ink, since the Rodez inmates would knock it over his writings and books. Artaud's concerns ranged from his past life to the new excremental language he was now formulating; he placed special emphasis on the capacity of this language to attack priests, such as the Bishop of Rodez. It was a language that emerged from 'a tetanus of the soul',[38] and from a process of grinding anatomical suffering. For Artaud, this substance of physical debris and fragmentation could become a universally transmissible language. He tried to persuade Parisot that he had already used this language in the past:

> In 1934 I wrote an entire book in this way, in a language which everybody could read, whatever nationality they belonged to. Unfortunately, this book has been lost. Only a very few copies were printed, and the abominable influences of people in government, in the church, or in the police intervened to make them disappear. There is only one copy left, which I don't have, but which stayed in the hands of one of my daughters: Catherine Chilé.[39]

With Artaud's permission, Parisot collected together the letters he had been sent, to publish them under the title *Letters from Rodez*.

Artaud continued to receive visitors. On 26 February 1946, the young writers Arthur Adamov and Marthe Robert came to Rodez to see Artaud, and to discuss his release with Ferdière. They had known Artaud before his departure from Ireland, and told him stories about how he had outrageously insulted people in the Montparnasse cafés, which made Artaud very happy. Adamov talked to

Artaud of a plan to republish all his books with Gallimard. Artaud was eagerly looking forward to his release from Rodez as 'the explosion of a dead volcano'.[40] But Ferdière exacted two conditions for Artaud's release: that he should live in a nursing home, and that he had to be financially secure. When Adamov returned to Paris, he collected a huge quantity of donated manuscripts and paintings – works by Georges Bataille, Simone de Beauvoir, Jean-Paul Sartre, Pablo Picasso, Georges Braque, Alberto Giacometti, Henri Michaux, and many others – to be auctioned to provide money for Artaud. Roger Blin began to organize a theatre event for Artaud's benefit. Neither the auction nor the theatre performance took place before Artaud's release, but the plans succeeded in reassuring Ferdière. Adamov gave the task of finding a suitable nursing home to a young woman named Paule Thévenin, whose husband was a doctor; she chose Dr Achille Delmas's convalescence clinic in the south-eastern suburbs of Paris, at Ivry-sur-Seine.

Despite the visit, Artaud was still feeling desperately isolated; on the day Adamov and Marthe Robert left Rodez, he wrote to Anie Besnard (who had not replied to any of his letters for three years):

> You can't imagine how much I miss here – and in my life – a friendship such as you showed me in 1937 at 21 rue Daguerre before your departure for Corsica. I am always so alone, with never a heart nor an affection such as I feel for you, and nobody to follow me as on that brilliant August afternoon when, in an ochre dress and a green turban, you followed me on a visit to the Gradiva gallery and to an exhibition where there were drawings by Sonia Mossé. Who is now dead in a concentration camp. All my best friends have either died or disappeared. Yvonne Allendy, Catherine Chilé, Neneka, Ana Corbin. I am alone.[41]

It was to this letter, passed on personally to Anie Besnard by Marthe Robert, that Artaud finally received the reply he wanted.

Artaud had been corresponding since the beginning of 1945 with a young novelist named Henri Thomas, about an article Thomas was writing on *The Theatre and its Double*; on 10 March Thomas came to Rodez to meet Artaud, along with his wife Colette, who was an actress. Artaud had already told Thomas that his work was still as virulent as it had been in the Surrealist years: 'My situation is that of the man who wrote the *Address to the Pope* in issue 3 of *La Révolution surréaliste*, the *Domestic Letters* and several other invective letters against priests, police and society, and whom they

wanted to silence forever because he refused to back down on
certain points as Aragon and Éluard had.'⁴² Artaud was extremely
happy with the visit; he introduced Henri and Colette Thomas to
Jean Dequeker, and read poems by Gérard de Nerval to them. He
felt an empathy with Henri Thomas, and told him that he was
conscious of all the upheavals in the world – war, famine, German
and Russian extermination camps – that had come about since his
internment in 1937. After Thomas had returned to Paris, Artaud
wrote to confide in him the reasons why the Theatre of Cruelty had
disintegrated: 'In this way I had terrible trouble in writing and
publishing *The Theatre and its Double*, which in 1933 announced
and desired war, famine and plague. But it was almost impossible
for me to stage and to perform a spectacle. That always ended up in
scandal, screams, police, and no spectators.'⁴³

Artaud was attracted by Colette Thomas (whose marriage was
unsteady); his feelings for her would extend beyond the time of his
internment. For Artaud, she seemed to embody his new life and
coming liberation. He was still alive in the face of ill will and a great
collective forgetting of him. Though his health had been shattered
by the asylum and electroshocks, and his face was toothless, Artaud
believed he could be resuscitated with the help of 'immortal young
girls'⁴⁴ such as Colette Thomas, who was about twenty-four at this
time. He began to incorporate her into his 'daughters of the heart'.
Colette Thomas had also suffered asylum treatments after being
interned in the mental hospital at Caen during her student years;
she had been placed in a strait-jacket and given cardiazol, a seizure-
provoking drug generally administered as a prelude to electroshock. (Colette Thomas's mental condition deteriorated in later
years, until she was in such a state of mental bewilderment that she
could no longer even remember Artaud.)⁴⁵ Naturally Artaud had
immense sympathy for her. During the final part of his internment,
he and Colette Thomas wrote many times to each other. Artaud
included his letters in a book entitled *Henchmen and Torturings*
which he was beginning to plan at this point, and Colette Thomas
used fragments from her letters in the first part of her only book,
published in 1954, *The Testament of the Dead Daughter*. In this
work, now almost forgotten, Colette Thomas interrogated her
ideas of solitude, separation and sexual catastrophe. She also described how she felt at being included within the volatile, transforming system of Artaud's daughters: 'If you do not want me to be

one of your actresses I will be one of your soldiers. If you do not want me to be one of your soldiers I will be one of your daughters. If you do not want me to be one of your daughters I will be your Unique daughter.'[46]

During his last months at Rodez Artaud was writing constantly. In addition to his exercise-book fragments, he produced a fierce article for the Marseilles-based magazine *Les Cahiers du Sud* on Isidore Ducasse, who wrote *Maldoror*, the book which had been crucial to the ideas of the Surrealists. Ducasse – who used the pseudonym 'Comte de Lautréamont' – had died in obscurity at the age of twenty-four, in 1870. Artaud presented his death as the result of a vicious social suppression which had also caused the suicides of many of the writers he felt solidarity with, such as Edgar Allan Poe and Gérard de Nerval; the following year, he turned this investigation to the death of Vincent Van Gogh. Artaud was also planning a book, suggested by Adamov, which would include the Ducasse article, a dream description, and a text composed of fragments. The book's provisional title, *For the Poor Popocatepel*, pointed to Artaud's identification with the Mexican volcano, and paralleled its potential explosivity with that of his own body as it neared its liberation from Rodez. He also used the story of Christ's crucifixion as a ready-made narrative to rework this imagery of a body which could eruptively resuscitate itself. In the case of Artaud's Christ (who was named Artaud and had an enemy named Nalpas), this physical reworking would happen 'without the intervention of a god, of a jesus-christ or of a spirit'.[47] In Artaud's crucifixion narrative, he burst with rage as he came alive again, scattering the soldiers around him just as he had scattered his assailants when he returned from Ireland on the *Washington* in September 1937.

In March 1946, a writer named André de Richaud arrived for a stay at the asylum of Rodez. He had been a brilliant, precocious novelist and playwright at the beginning of the 1930s, but now suffered from incapacitating alcoholism and drug addiction. Artaud knew Richaud's work (he had considered staging it for the Alfred Jarry Theatre), and Ferdière decided to give Artaud a trial release by sending him to stay with Richaud at a hotel in the nearby town of Espalion. Richaud could supervise Artaud, and Artaud could watch over Richaud's alcohol consumption. Ferdière promised Artaud that after this trial release, he could return to Paris. Artaud and Richaud left for Espalion on 19 March. Artaud registered the fact that he was being given a mentor who was also an unstable drug addict, and was acutely conscious of the many contradictions in Ferdière's position towards him. He wrote in his exercise-books of how Ferdière had welcomed him to Rodez, but had then given him electroshocks; how he had encouraged him to write again, but had then forbidden him to chant what he had produced.

At Espalion, away from Ferdière's control, Artaud immediately became anxious to have drugs again; he wrote to his friends in Paris, and even to his sister, asking them to send him heroin or codeine. He enjoyed the independence of his life at Espalion, and wrote to Dequeker: 'The countryside here is just what I've been looking for after 9 years of internment. Silent, with nobody who is astonished by my face. My appearance is that of a man who has suffered much, and there are so many idiots.'[48] Richaud was behaving well, taking long walks and watching football matches, and Artaud was able to work. He wrote to Roger Blin that his first project upon returning to Paris would be to set the Theatre of Cruelty into movement again: 'I need actors who are first of all beings, that is to say that when they are on stage, they won't be afraid of the true sensation of a knife-wound . . .'[49] He also completed the text of fragments to send to Adamov, and entitled it *Fragmentations*. In this text, he constructed a rigorous architecture of interactive fragments to produce an incisive imagery of the violence he had suffered, and the counterattacks he was preparing with his 'daughters of the heart', Marthe Robert and Colette Thomas:

> And I saw Marthe Robert in Paris, I saw her from Rodez to Paris, leaning forward with rage in the corner of my locked room, just in front of my night table, like a flower uprooted by anger, in the apocalypse of life.
> And there is also Colette Thomas, to blow the police of hatred from Paris to Nagasaki.
> She will explain to you her own tragedy.[50]

It was to be Colette Thomas herself who delivered these fragments during the readings of Artaud's texts at the theatre benefit performance of 7 June.

At Rodez, Ferdière was having administrative problems in arranging for Artaud's release. A row arose over the royalties which had arrived for Artaud's book *Letters from Rodez*, which was published in April. Ferdière had strongly disapproved of the book and had tried to prevent its appearance; now, the asylum's administrator wanted to seize the money – which Artaud needed to pay his hotel bill at Espalion and for his journey to Paris – as a contribution towards the cost of his treatments at the asylum. This infuriated Artaud, since they had not been treatments of his choosing, and his internment had been compulsory in the first place. On 10 April, Ferdière sent the asylum's ambulance and two psychiatric nurses to bring Artaud back from Espalion.

These difficulties were temporary, however, and the date of 25 May was set for Artaud's release. He was still terrified of the possibility of more electroshocks, and was concerned that Ferdière was to accompany him back to Paris. Ferdière had two patients to escort to Sainte-Anne, and Artaud feared that his release would turn out only to be a disguised transfer to another asylum. But Ferdière was now ready to show his rehabilitated patient to the Parisian literary world. In the days leading up to his release, Artaud wrote to his friends, asking them to meet him on the evening of his arrival in Paris. For the meeting place, he chose the Café de Flore in Saint Germain-des-Prés, which was to become one of the principal creative sites of the final period of his life. A young poet named Jacques Prevel had written to him and sent him some of his work, and Artaud had also received a visit from another writer from Paris, Alain Berne-Joffroy, who was visiting his family near Rodez and took the opportunity to call in on Artaud. The idea of staying at Dr Delmas's clinic was disconcerting for Artaud – he wanted now to avoid 'the atmosphere of sickness',[51] and would have preferred a hotel. But he had no choice. He packed his drawings and exercise-books for the journey.

On Saturday, 25 May, Ferdière wrote a release certificate and a final diagnosis: 'Displays a chronic, very longstanding delirium; for several months, there has been the absence of violent reactions, his conduct is much more coherent, takes care of his appearance, etc. . . .; it seems that an attempt at re-adaptation is now possible.' Photographs were taken of Artaud sitting on a bench in the asylum grounds with Ferdière, Dequeker and the head nurse, Adrienne Régis. Artaud, now almost fifty years old, had aged terribly during his three years at Rodez, since the photograph had been taken of his face with its cropped hair and fearful eyes on his arrival from Ville-Évrard. Artaud and Ferdière took the night train to Paris, arriving at the Gare d'Austerlitz at dawn on 26 May 1946.

5

Ivry – Blows and Bombs

When Artaud arrived at the Gare d'Austerlitz in Paris and shook hands with Ferdière for the last time, he had twenty-two months still to live. The amount and intensity of work he was to accomplish in that time proved to be enormous. Until that point, Artaud had largely been preoccupied with each of his activities separately: writing, drawing, theatre direction, film projects and acting, and drug intoxication. This changed completely in the last period of his life. Certainly aware that he was pressed for time, he worked constantly, night and day, in all situations and surroundings – on metro trains, in cafés, while eating, while taking drugs. Only the drug comas of the last year of his life began to punch holes into his ferocious rhythm of work. He compacted the various layers of his work together, so that drawings entered his texts and texts entered his drawings; in his recorded work, screams and cries entered the written texts he was performing, and silences entered the screams. Much of Artaud's work was now made up of gestures. He believed that gesture and dance would remake his broken body, and all his creative acts were surrounded and penetrated by violent gestures – made, then immediately lost. Sometimes the sense of gesture in Artaud's last work can be rediscovered, stuck into the surface of his drawings, or within his recorded scream. It was during these last years, 1946 to 1948, that Artaud came closest to realizing the ideas of urgent, burning gesture which are embedded in *The Theatre and its Double*. The last part of Artaud's life had no respite: it was relentlessly incendiary and furious. Artaud intended to produce new images of the human body, and did so. He wrote through extreme illness, ridicule and addiction, until he felt that he had said all that it was crucial for him to say; at that point, he died.

Several of Artaud's friends were waiting for him at the station in the early morning of 26 May 1946: Jean Dubuffet, Marthe Robert, and Henri and Colette Thomas. (Jacques Prevel, the poet who had written to Artaud at Rodez and was anxious to meet him, intended to be there but failed to get out of bed in time.) Artaud's friends took him to Dr Delmas's clinic in the rue de la Mairie (now the rue de Lénine) in Ivry-sur-Seine, where he was given a room in a new pavilion. The clinic was a convalescent and nursing home, not an asylum, and Artaud was delighted with the kind welcome given to him by Dr Delmas, who also treated James Joyce's daughter Lucia (Joyce and Samuel Beckett visited her at the clinic in Ivry). Delmas handed Artaud a set of keys to the clinic gates in order to reassure him that he was not being incarcerated in a closed institution, and could come and go as he pleased. On one occasion, Artaud returned to the clinic late at night having forgotten his keys, and had to be helped over the high wall by two policemen. It was a private clinic, set in an extensive wooded parkland, close to the railway tracks on which Artaud had travelled back from Rodez. The fees were high, but Artaud's financial situation was assured throughout the rest of his life from the profits of the auction of manuscripts and the theatre benefit performance. Dubuffet administered these funds and paid the clinic fees out of them. (Dubuffet was succeeded in this role by Jean Paulhan and Pierre Loeb.) Artaud received a sum of money, roughly equivalent to the wage of a manual worker of the time, for his personal use. Delmas became aware of the gestures and cries with which Artaud punctuated his writing, and installed a huge block of wood in his room. Artaud struck it with hammers, pokers and knives, finally reducing it to splinters as he tested the rhythms for the poems he was working on. In the evening of his first day in Paris, he walked the streets with Henri Thomas; Paris gave Artaud 'an impression of the void'.[1] He was searching for the apartments of friends who had died, or whom he had invented. Henri Thomas finally took him to see André Gide, who had recently returned to Paris after an absence of six years. Artaud recited 'a very beautiful poem of dereliction and fury'[2] for Gide, who wept. Artaud began to believe that his return to Paris would go well.

Great upheavals in Parisian life and culture had taken place since Artaud had last been there. After the Liberation from the German Occupation in 1944, the important intellectual figures were men such as Albert Camus and Jean-Paul Sartre, both of whom had worked for the Resistance and consequently gained an aura of heroic commitment. Conditions in the city were still grim in 1946. Frequent electricity cuts interrupted the metro, many foods were scarce, the black market was pervasive, and much of Paris's

population was preoccupied with accusing their enemies of collaboration with the Germans during the Occupation. The Surrealist
movement attracted little more than feelings of indifference or
hostility at this time. André Breton had been absent from the
struggle against the Occupation and had spent the war years principally in New York, along with a number of the other Surrealists.
Artaud wrote to Breton, who arrived back in Paris five days after
him: 'I, Antonin Artaud, do not want to shoot you in the legs at a
moment when everybody else is doing it . . .'³ Artaud largely
escaped this animosity, since his Surrealist texts were now long out
of print, and he had been expelled from the movement almost
twenty years previously. He was known principally for *The Theatre
and its Double*, which had been re-issued in 1944, and the *Letters
from Rodez*, which had provoked an impact of disturbed awe on
their publication in April 1946. Artaud's internment was a source of
great sympathy and indignation. The writer Jacques Prévert told
Roger Blin that what Artaud had lived through was 'worse than
deportation' to a concentration camp.⁴

Despite the austerity of post-war Paris, a vivid sense of artistic
experimentation and rediscovery had flared up after the Liberation.
In 1946, Nico Papatakis opened his Existentialist nightclub 'La
Rose Rouge' in the new artistic axis of Saint Germain-des-Prés.
Many emergent artistic groups were now demanding attention. The
Lettrists, led by Isidore Isou, were working enthusiastically with
disintegrated elements of language. (Isou met Artaud during this
period at the Flore and found him 'extremely disappointing in his
appearance and his behaviour'.)⁵ The COBRA group, notably
Karel Appel, put together violently coloured, clumsy paintings and
sculptures which resembled those of children. At this time, Dubuffet was initiating his ideas for 'Art Brut', a concept which gave
prominence to the creative work of asylum patients and uneducated
people. There had been an explosion of small-scale independent
publishing after the Liberation, directed by young writers such as
Adamov and Thomas who were seeking outlets for their work.
Artaud always demonstrated a certain hostility towards the culture
around him – he told Jacques Prevel 'When I hear people talking
about a new poet, I want to shoot him at pointblank range'⁶ – but it
would be largely through these new outlets that his last writings
appeared.

Artaud went into Paris daily to meet his friends in the Saint
Germain-des-Prés cafés, especially the Flore. He caught the metro

from Ivry each morning after he had been brought breakfast in his room and had been shaved by the barber in the rue de la Mairie. The friends he saw most of during this period were Adamov and Blin (whom Artaud included in his crucifixion story as the Good Thief crucified alongside him). He became attached to Jacques Prevel after meeting him on the day following his arrival back in Paris. Prevel was ill with tuberculosis; he lived in wretched poverty and wrote poems about his incapacity to write poems. He became one of Artaud's closest associates, and kept a journal in which he recorded all their meetings. (It was published in 1974 under the title *In the Company of Antonin Artaud*.) He regularly submitted his poems for Artaud's appraisal, hoping that he would show them to Jean Paulhan. Although *La Nouvelle Revue Française* had been officially suspended (after Gaston Gallimard was unfairly accused of collaboration) and was not published during the last part of Artaud's life, Paulhan remained a dominant figure in the Parisian literary milieu. Artaud began taking copious amounts of laudanum again after his return to Paris, and he constantly asked Prevel to procure it for him. Prevel spent much of his time with Artaud at Ivry, and on one occasion Artaud demanded that Prevel participate in his cries. Prevel reported what happened in his journal. Artaud said to him:

> 'You will not leave this room alive if you do not answer me.'
> And he stuck his knife straight into the table. So I started to shout with him. It relieved me, since I had been hearing him doing it for two hours and I felt the need to do it myself.
> 'You have done something very remarkable,' he told me immediately afterwards. 'If we had been on a stage, we would have been a great success.'[7]

Artaud met Breton for the first time since 1937 on 1 June, the day after Breton's return to Paris. It was a clash of opposed commitments. Artaud wanted Breton to verify his hallucinations about the circumstances of his arrest in September 1937, while Breton patronizingly told Artaud that his adventures had been like a story by Gérard de Nerval. Over the months that followed, they saw each other often in Saint Germain-des-Prés. The same divergences that had caused their split in 1926 and Artaud's expulsion from the Surrealist movement now returned with renewed force. Breton was diminished in Artaud's eyes because he would not take Artaud's claims seriously. Artaud would tell Prevel: 'If you dug a little bit into the world of André Breton with a spiked stick, you would find worms.'[8]

On 5 June, Paule Thévenin – the woman whom Adamov had asked to find a suitable clinic for Artaud – went to meet him for the first time at Ivry-sur-Seine. She was living nearby, over the river in Charenton. Paule Thévenin was about twenty-four at this time; she had been a medical student and had also considered acting. She had a young daughter named Domnine and had called with her at Ivry on the previous day, while Artaud was out. A friend of Paule Thévenin named Gervais Marchal had suggested that Artaud should do a reading for the literary radio programme *Club d'Essai*, which had been started under the Occupation in 1942, as an outlet for experimental material. Paule Thévenin went to ask Artaud if he would like to make such a recording. At first Artaud was suspicious of the radio station's official aura, and sceptical that he would be allowed to read exactly what he wanted, but Paule Thévenin reassured him. He liked Paule Thévenin, and immediately incorporated her into his 'daughters of the heart'. She would be the last woman to be included in that volatile arrangement. They became close friends, and Artaud often made the journey to Charenton to see her. On one occasion he brought her a huge bouquet of flowers, which he had put together as an evocation of her consciousness. Artaud preferred to dictate his texts, especially for their final version. Paule Thévenin learned how to take his dictation, and typed out his virtually illegible manuscripts.

Artaud immediately set to work on writing the text for radio transmission. The recording session was only two days away. He produced a text which advocated his belief in the superiority of an 'anti-social' state of sickness, over a 'social' state of health supported by doctors and human cowardice. His sickness, 'beautiful only because it is terrible',[9] would be powerful since it was reinforced by fevers that came from opium, heroin and cocaine. Artaud recorded his provocative text, 'The Patients and the doctors', on the morning of 8 June. Giving his words a strong rhythmic emphasis, he included elements from his invented language. When he listened to the recording, which was broadcast on the following day, he believed that he sounded like an over-dramatic classical actor, and was horrified. The evening before the recording session, the theatre benefit event organized by Roger Blin had taken place. Breton had made his first public appearance since his return to Paris and had introduced the event. Despite her nervous

terror of the occasion, Colette Thomas performed *Fragmentations* to
great applause, and there were other readings by actors such as
Roger Blin (who performed *The New Revelations of Being*), Louis
Jouvet, Charles Dullin, and Jean-Louis Barrault, who later denied
that he had appeared. Artaud was not allowed to attend, despite his
great desire to do so, since Breton, Adamov and Marthe Robert
decided it would be too much of a shock for him. On 13 June the
sale was held of the donated manuscripts and paintings; the actor
Pierre Brasseur served as the auctioneer, assisted by Anie Besnard.
Many collectors were present, and a sum of over one million francs
was raised for Artaud.

Artaud was now writing a great deal of poetry, for the first time
since the Surrealist years. Much of it concerned his return to Paris
as someone who was perceived socially as a madman or fanatic. He
began to put together a collection of poems entitled *Artaud the
Mômo – mômo* was a Marseilles slang word for a fool or village idiot;
for Artaud, the word had resonances of many other things, notably
mummification and childishness. For these poems, Artaud
developed a language which used many violent, excremental and
sexual terms; he also soldered words together, and visually
emphasized the parts of his poems where he worked with his
invented language of incantation. This language was intended to be
read aloud and to create immediate sonic impacts, rather than to
function through the resemblance of its components to words in the
French language (or the Greek, Italian, German and English languages, which were also fed into Artaud's linguistic furnace):

> **klaver striva**
> **cavour tavina**
> **scaver kavina**
> **okar triva**[10]

Artaud wanted to reach a wide, non-intellectual audience with his
writings. For this reason, he was attracted to the idea of broad-
casting his work on the radio, and also to having it appear in
mass-circulation newspapers. He wrote a text entitled 'Madness
and black magic', which condemned the institution of mental hospitals – he saw them as factories of magical torture. They were
instruments of social suppression, and used electroshocks to pacify
their victims' desire for revolution. In this text, Artaud used a style
that was rhythmic, flexible and journalistically paced. He sent
'Madness and black magic' to two newspapers, *Combat* (which had

been started by the Resistance fighters in Paris and had Albert Camus as one of its leading figures) and *Franc-Tireur*. They both turned it down. He had been planning to read 'The Patients and the doctors' again on the radio for the *Club d'Essai* programme, since he had been so dissatisfied with his first attempt. Now he changed his mind and performed 'Madness and black magic' instead, on 16 July (it was transmitted on the following day). Artaud also included it among the poetic texts he was writing for *Artaud the Mômo*, and added a section on the Tarahumara Indians. The book's publisher, Pierre Bordas, wanted Artaud to persuade Pablo Picasso to illustrate his poems. Artaud arranged numerous appointments with Picasso, who avoided them all. In exasperation, Artaud decided to illustrate the book himself with the drawings he was including in his exercise-books. These drawings were used to punctuate the fragmentary exercise-book texts and to demonstrate what Artaud was writing about with greater visual immediacy – the drawings were of nails, skulls and dancing bodies. He told Bordas that the book would gain force from the incorporation of his 'totems' and 'mysterious, operating machines'.[11] He was also being asked to write new texts by many people, particularly the young writers who had started their own magazines. On 8 July, with his customary rapidity of the time, he wrote a text for Michel Hincker entitled 'The Theatre and the Anatomy', which explored his ideas of how physical and theatrical spaces should be meshed.

Artaud was offered a contract by Gaston Gallimard on 1 August for the publication of the play he had staged for the Theatre of Cruelty in 1935, *The Cenci*. Gallimard was also proposing to publish all Artaud's previous writings in the form of a *Collected Works*; this put Artaud into a state of intense activity all through August, making lists of the books he particularly wanted to be re-published. He also began to write new versions of the Surrealist open letters from 1925 to give them a contemporary relevance and incision. He intended to erase their mystical aspects, and to include the events of the intervening twenty years of his life. Two of these open letters, to the Pope and the Dalai Lama, would be completed later in the year. Also during August, Artaud wrote an introduction for the *Collected Works*. It ranged over his life and work from the time of his arguments with Jacques Rivière, through to his creation of the murdered 'daughters of the heart to be born' and his new concept of cruelty:

The theatre is the scaffold, the gallows, the trenches, the crematorium oven or the lunatic asylum.

Cruelty: massacred bodies.[12]

He was quickly becoming disillusioned with his new 'daughters of the heart' – in his perception, Colette Thomas had already been divided between a double who existed and whom he had met in his life, and a true Colette who was yet to appear. He resented Marthe Robert's liaison with Adamov. Anie Besnard was now married, and Artaud furiously demanded that she provide proof of her fidelity to him alone, and that she reject her husband and family, whom he regarded as 'bastards' who had seduced her with money:

> I have no money but
> I am
> *Antonin Artaud*
> and I can be rich, immensely and *immediately* rich
> if I only wanted to make the effort. The trouble is that I have
> always had a hatred for money, for fortune, for wealth . . .[13]

On 20 August, Artaud began his new series of drawings with a portrait of Prevel's wife, Rolande. He had previously drawn a strange human figure as part of a dedication to Paule Thévenin, inscribed in her copy of *The Theatre and its Double* in June. In his drawings from August 1946 onward, Artaud worked almost exclusively on the face, drawing portraits of all his friends and the people who came to see him at Ivry. For the next nine months he concentrated a delicate but fiery energy into transforming the faces of the people in his drawings. He tried to execute a bursting of the facial flesh on the surface of the paper; at the same time, he consciously aimed to collapse the aesthetic value attached to the unified physical form and its representation. He dissolved and concurrently restructured the face, attempting to get inside its material and to remake it. In these portraits, he cut open a space where a multiplicity of controlled forces was set to work on the image, tearing and harassing it, while also breaking it open for potential physical realignment. Artaud scarred his drawings of the face with the evidence of gesture, cancelling and marking the face with his reactivated strength, working to break down what he saw as its layers and screens, until it attained its authentic appearance.

Artaud travelled down to the south of France by train on the night of 13 September for a holiday at Sainte-Maxime. Marthe Robert went with him, and stayed at the same hotel. Paule

Thévenin and Colette Thomas followed them to the Mediterranean coast on the next day and stayed in a sea-front villa owned by Colette Thomas's aunt at La Nartelle, close to Sainte-Maxime. At the end of July, Colette Thomas had had an aesthetic operation, paid for by Artaud, to remove some bones in her feet and make them smaller, and she had been convalescing at Paule Thévenin's house. Artaud was able to see Paule Thévenin and Colette Thomas every day. Surrounded by his 'daughters of the heart', he wrote a great amount of new material in Sainte-Maxime. He produced a text entitled 'Beat and Hammer' in which he declared his contempt for written language: 'In reality I say nothing and I do nothing. I use neither words nor letters, *I never use words and I never even use letters*.'[14] Now, his language would be expressed 'by blows and by screams'.[15] Part of Artaud's time was spent in seeing doctors who could prescribe laudanum for him, and in contacting friends in Paris such as Prevel to ask them to send him drugs. The stay in Sainte-Maxime went well, apart from Dubuffet's initial refusal to release money from Artaud's funds to enable him to pay Marthe Robert's hotel bill as well as his own. They returned to Paris on 4 October.

One day soon after arriving back in Paris from Sainte-Maxime, Artaud took a walk in the grounds of the clinic at Ivry, and found a large derelict hunting pavilion deep in the woods. It dated from the eighteenth century, and its french windows opened out into a garden of flowers. Artaud decided that he wanted to leave his new room and live in this pavilion instead. It had no running water, electricity or central heating, and at first Dr Delmas tried to dissuade him. But Artaud insisted: he wanted a sense of isolation from the other inhabitants of the clinic. Delmas arranged for the gardener to bring Artaud jugs of water and logs for the huge fireplace, which Artaud liked to say was the only luxury in his pavilion. Delmas also wanted to install central heating, but Artaud refused to move out long enough for it to be done. The pavilion consisted of two rooms, one of which was very large and gave him space for his drawing, dancing and gestural movements. After so many constrictive hotel rooms and asylum cells, Artaud became attached to his new accommodation; he soon elaborated a story that it was a pavilion in which the poet Gérard de Nerval had once stayed. Artaud would live there until his death.

Artaud was now receiving frequent requests for texts, and offers of collaboration with other writers. In September 1946, both

Artaud and the young poet Henri Pichette – who would become renowned a year later with the production of his play *The Epiphanies* – had texts refused by the magazine *Arts et Lettres*. The sub-editor who had commissioned Artaud's text, Bernard Lucas, resigned from the magazine and published the rejected texts of Artaud and Pichette together in a booklet issued in fifty copies, entitled by Artaud *Xylophony against the Popular Press and its Little Audience*. This made Prevel jealous, since he wanted to be seen as collaborating with Artaud. Adamov's first book *The Confession*, about sexual humiliation and despair, was published by Gallimard soon after Artaud's release from Rodez; in October, Artaud wrote a text entitled 'The Untimely Death and the Confession of Arthur Adamov' for Paulhan's magazine *Les Cahiers de la Pléiade*, to signal the appearance of Adamov's book. He wrote that *The Confession* 'weeps the prenatal assassination of poetry',[16] and formulated a denunciation of death as a kind of socially inspired deformation of the body. Henri Parisot had been in touch with Artaud again, and requested that Artaud write an introduction for his translations of the work of Samuel Taylor Coleridge. Artaud read Coleridge's poetry, but disliked it and delayed completing his text until 17 November, by which time it was too late to be included with Parisot's translations. In 'Coleridge the Traitor', Artaud created a vision of a virulent poetry composed of blood, mucous, cruelty and insurrection. He believed that in all of Coleridge's work, only an early fragment (probably 'Reality's Dark Dream' from 1803) possessed these qualities. In Artaud's view, Coleridge had subsequently become scared of his poetic power and had, as a result, lost his claim to a literal physical immortality. Despite the fact that Coleridge, too, had taken opium, Artaud largely overlooked that aspect of his life. He simply asserted that Coleridge's vital poems had survived solely through their distillation into opium.

Towards the end of 1946, Artaud was working at a furious pace. He produced two long and intricate poems, *Here Lies* and *The Indian Culture*, during the course of one burst of writing on 25 November. He arranged for these two poems to be published together in one volume by a small company, K, run by Parisot and Alain Gheerbrandt. K was one of the numerous French publishers to reject Samuel Beckett's novels during these years. All Artaud's books of the last period suffered long delays before they appeared, largely due to the financial precariousness of the publishing companies involved, and their desire to wait and see how much interest

Artaud's return to Paris generated. Much to Artaud's dismay, his poetry was to appear in expensive luxury editions of several hundred copies, rather than in the massive, accessible editions which he demanded.

Artaud was working on a new book, *Henchmen and Torturings*; it had evolved from the idea suggested by Adamov, while Artaud was still at Rodez, for the project which had been provisionally titled *For the Poor Popocatepel*. Artaud included many of his recent letters in this book, especially those to his new friends and 'daughters of the heart', and to well-known figures such as Breton and Georges Braque. The book was intended to form a bridge between Artaud's incarceration at Rodez and his new life in Paris, and he wanted it to demonstrate his current preoccupations. He signed a contract for the book with Louis Broder and the gallery owner Pierre Loeb, who was renowned for promoting the work of the Surrealists and of artists such as Balthus. Loeb hired a secretary and sent her to Ivry each morning from the end of November 1946 to 8 February 1947, so that Artaud could dictate a sequence of new texts to be included in the book. He was usually still in bed when she arrived at the pavilion, and he remained there, simultaneously eating his breakfast and spitting out violent text after text from his toothless mouth. He spoke of how malicious beings came to attack him every night and drink his sperm; how he hated sexuality and all the organs of the body – especially the tongue and the heart, which would have to be excised before a true body of shattered bone and nerve could be created; how he opposed all religions; and how, faced with so many assaults, his brain went 'up in smoke as under the action of one of those machines created to suck up filth from the floor'.[17] When Broder read this material, he suffered a religious crisis and refused to publish the book. The project then passed through the hands of two of Artaud's other publishers, Pierre Bordas and K. Fragmented and inflammatory on a massive scale, *Henchmen and Torturings* was not published until thirty years after Artaud's death. He said himself that it was 'absolutely impossible to read' and that 'nobody has ever read it from end to end, not even its author'.[18]

Throughout his first six months back in Paris, Artaud was considering staging a spectacle that would bring the Theatre of Cruelty back to life. He was contemplating a performance which could be an amalgam of screams and violence, and he initially planned to stage Euripides' *The Bacchantes*. But his concept of performance had been transformed totally since the time of *The Cenci* in 1935, and Artaud quickly abandoned the idea of a spectacle which would have any appearance of theatre, and which would be dependent upon the susceptibilities of a group of actors who might disobey him to some degree. As Artaud had written to Roger Blin while still at Rodez, he needed actors who would literally bleed for the Theatre of Cruelty; Blin himself and Alain Cuny were the only actors who might have been prepared to do that for Artaud. So Artaud decided to confront his audience alone, on a bare stage, just as he had done at the Sorbonne in 1933, while preoccupied with the desire to express the impact of the plague on the body. The manager of a theatre in Saint Germain-des-Prés, the Vieux-Colombier, offered Artaud the opportunity to give his performance there; Adamov and the many young writers who were visiting Artaud at Ivry encouraged him to make this first public appearance since the Brussels lecture of 1937. Some of Artaud's contemporaries, especially Breton, expressed strong reservations about the performance, believing that Artaud was being exploited and put into a situation which would prove a destabilizing ordeal. But the event went ahead, and Artaud painstakingly prepared a text which would pin down all the assaults he had suffered in Mexico, in Ireland, and in the asylums. His many accusations would now be made public, reinforced by his physical presence.

Artaud's event, which he entitled *The Story Lived by Artaud-Mômo*, took place on the evening of 13 January 1947. The theatre was crowded with nine hundred spectators, most of whom were young people; several hundred latecomers had to be turned away when the theatre became too packed. Numerous friends from all periods of Artaud's life in Paris were present at the Vieux-Colombier, including André Gide, Jean Paulhan, Roger Blin and Arthur Adamov; Albert Camus and Georges Braque also attended. Despite his reservations, André Breton went to Artaud's performance and sat at the back of the theatre. Since no sound recording was made of what Artaud said, the most valuable accounts of the event are those by people who wrote down their impressions immediately afterwards, notably Prevel and the journalist Maurice Saillet, whose review appeared in *Combat* on 24 January. Artaud appeared on stage with a mass of papers which made up his prepared text. He spoke for three hours altogether, from nine until midnight; at first he was heckled, but Artaud silenced the interruptions with his magisterial gravity. After that, the performance continued with the audience in absolute silence. The heat in the small theatre caused people to faint. Artaud was in a highly charged, strained state, and began by reading three poems – two from the collection *Artaud the Mômo*, and *The Indian Culture*. His delivery was shredded with silences, and his hands fluttered nervously around his face and gripped it. The poems were almost inaudible, sobbed and stammered out into the room as fragments from Artaud's survival. According to Prevel, Artaud also performed 'Madness and black magic', with greater coherence. After reading the poems, Artaud stopped dead; an interval was called, and Gide climbed up on to the stage to embrace him.

Artaud opened the second half of his performance by starting to read his prepared text. It was concerned particularly with the denial of death which Artaud was formulating at this time. For Artaud, death was always an invented state, imposed by society so that the inert body would become vulnerable raw material for malicious robberies and attacks as it entered a state of limbo, such as he claimed to have experienced during an electroshock coma at Rodez. With a strong enough will to live, and sufficient resistance to social compromise, an independent human body could live forever, powered by anger. But Artaud did not get this far with his reading. He dropped his papers on the floor, and stood acutely exposed, as though paralysed. A long, agonized silence followed; Artaud would later write to Maurice Saillet that 'what I had to say was in my silences, not in my words'.[19] When he spoke again, it was to begin a wild improvisation, constantly shattered by cries, screams and savage gestures. He ferociously denounced his electroshock treatments at Rodez, accusing Ferdière by name, and constructed fractured narratives of the journeys to Mexico and Ireland which he had undertaken ten years previously. He continued to spit out his fury and incant his stories for two hours. Finally, when he tried to convince the horrified and incredulous audience that he was the victim of a black magic bewitchment, Artaud knew that he had reached a dead-end. He said: 'I put myself in your place, and I see very well that what I am saying isn't interesting at all, it's still theatre. What can I do to be truly sincere?' He stopped again, and read a last poem from *Artaud the Mômo*. When he came to the words 'the filthy carcass', he aimed them directly at his stunned audience. Then Artaud abruptly left the stage.

Afterwards, Breton told Artaud that it was stupid of him to have undertaken such a performance. Since he had stood on the boards of a theatre, it proved that he was still a 'man of the theatre', as he

had been in 1926 when they had quarrelled over the Alfred Jarry
Theatre. Although Artaud had grasped that he could not penetrate
through from theatre to life, and had declared this on stage, what
Breton said infuriated him. At the same time, Breton invited
Artaud to participate – with either drawings or a catalogue text – in
the International Exhibition of Surrealism which he and Marcel
Duchamp were organizing at the Galerie Maeght in Paris for the
summer of 1947. Breton had decided to use the gallery space to
convey a kind of magical initiation in stages. The exhibition would
include rooms dedicated to voodoo, the tarot, and the zodiac. These
things were now anathema for Artaud, and he refused Breton's
request:

> André Breton, how can you do this? After reproaching me for
> appearing in a theatre, you invite me to participate in an exhibition,
> in an art gallery which is so chic, ultra-successful, affluent, capitalist
> (even though it has its account with a communist bank), and where
> all the exhibitions, whatever they are, can only have the stylized,
> limited, closed, fixed character of an attempt at art.[20]

For Artaud, the exhibition Breton was planning would be aimed
against himself personally, with malice, since its emphasis was on
the magical. And it would be useless for Breton to exhibit 'objects
which will not wail, reek, stink, fart, spit, will not show wounds,
will not receive them'.[21]

Artaud was convinced that his Vieux-Colombier performance
had not failed. He believed that it had demonstrated with great
immediacy and violence the potential of the new language of blows
and screams which he had conceived at Sainte-Maxime, and which
he was sure he would soon possess and wield. His experience at the
Vieux-Colombier had convinced him of the absolute necessity of
attacking society constantly, in all its forms. He wrote to Breton:

> No man of the theatre, in the entire history of the theatre, has
> previously taken the attitude which I had that night on stage at the
> Vieux-Colombier, which consisted of wailing out belches of hatred,
> colics and cramps to the limits of blackout, etc., etc.
>
> Besides gathering people together in a room, it remains for me to
> hurl abuse at this society in the street . . .[22]
>
> So yes, I appeared on a stage, *once again*, for the LAST TIME, at the
> Vieux-Colombier theatre, but with the visible intention of exploding
> its frame work, exploding its framework from inside, and I do not
> believe that the spectacle of a man who wails and yells fury to the

point of vomiting his intestines is a very theatrical spectacle . . .

I abandoned the stage because I realized the fact that the only language which I could have with an audience was to bring bombs out of my pockets and throw them in the audience's face with a blatant gesture of aggression . . . and blows are the only language in which I feel capable of speaking.[23]

Artaud's dispute with Breton was still essentially the same as it had been in 1926 – it was over the question of the presence of intention in the creative act, and about revolution and individual action against society. Artaud argued that although his performance had been wild and improvised, it had been so by intention. He lectured Breton on how Surrealism should work: it could only be revolutionary if it constantly interrogated and reinvented everything, from science and medicine to the human body itself. The recriminations continued by letter until May 1947; the final phase of Artaud's friendship with Breton was now exhausted. Despite his great desire, over the course of twenty years, for Breton to support and empathize with his work, Artaud finally could only push Breton away, to reinforce his own overwhelming sense of defiant individuality: 'I have my own idea of birth, of life, of death, of reality, of destiny, and I do not accept that someone can impose on me or suggest to me any other.'[24]

Towards the end of January 1947, Artaud was working on the final fragments of *Henchmen and Torturings*, which he had now been dictating for two months. Although Broder had by this time been scandalized by Artaud's work and wanted nothing more to do with it, Loeb continued to pay the secretary to receive Artaud's dictation every morning. A major exhibition of the paintings of Vincent Van Gogh opened at this time at the Orangerie museum in Paris, and Loeb wanted Artaud to write an essay about it. But Artaud was preoccupied with *Henchmen and Torturings*, which had now gone far beyond the limits of a publishable book of the time. Loeb finally provoked Artaud by sending him a newspaper cutting, in which a doctor diagnosed Van Gogh in a psychiatric vocabulary very close to that used to define Artaud's own mental condition at Ville-Évrard and Rodez. Van Gogh's working methods were treated as diagnostic indicators, to justify the doctor's position. Loeb's motivation was unsubtle: he wanted one asylum inmate to write on another. The article sent Artaud into a state of furious indignation. He quickly abandoned work on *Henchmen and Torturings* (he would return to it briefly at the end of February, but the book remained in a state of flux), and he asked Paule Thévenin to accompany him to the exhibition on 2 February. He had to go early in the morning and stayed only briefly, since the museum became intolerable to him when it filled with people – it was a Sunday. But he had seen enough of Van Gogh's paintings to generate the most renowned writing of his last years, *Van Gogh the Suicide of society*.

By the beginning of March the text had been completed and dictated to Paule Thévenin. For Artaud, the Van Gogh exhibition was a vital, eruptive event – the exact contrary to Breton's moribund Surrealist exhibition. Van Gogh's paintings were socially disruptive, dense objects which still shook nature and rearranged history. After the long and grinding process of writing *Henchmen and Torturings*, Artaud's language emerged as a lucid and infinitely flexible material in *Van Gogh the Suicide of society*. He could switch rapidly from vivid, journalistic passages which evoked the paintings with precision, to an imagery that compacted together Van Gogh's work and his own work on the raging human body:

> The body under the skin is an overheated factory
> and, outside,
> the sick man blazes,
> he glows,
> from all his burst pores.
> This is a landscape
> by Van Gogh
> at noon.[25]

As Pierre Loeb had anticipated, Artaud wrote about his own experiences in parallel to those of Van Gogh, just as he had written himself into the life of Heliogabalus in 1933. *Van Gogh the Suicide of society* became an arena in which Artaud worked over his bitterness towards the psychiatrists who had treated him. He described how he had felt the desire to commit suicide because he could not cut their throats. (Despite this, Ferdière spoke of *Van Gogh the Suicide of society* with great appreciation.) Artaud reserved his most venomous attack for Jacques Lacan, whom he derided as a 'filthy vile bastard'.[26] By this point, Artaud had formulated an entire group of poets and writers whose lives and work he allied to his own. They had all been driven to suicide or covertly murdered by a collective social will. In his letters to Breton, Artaud added Lenin to a list which always included the poets Nerval, Baudelaire and

Poe. For Artaud, every authentic act was driven by a sense of necessity or desperation: 'Nobody has ever written or painted, sculpted, modelled, constructed, invented, other than really to get out of hell.'[23] In *Van Gogh the Suicide of society*, Artaud also declared his belief in the 'authentic madman'. It was his own position during the previous ten years of internment, ridicule and struggle. He wrote of the madman: 'It is a man who has preferred to become mad, in the socially understood sense of the word, rather than betray a certain superior idea of human honour. . . . a madman is also a man whom society does not want to hear, and whom it wants to prevent from speaking intolerable truths.'[24] Artaud argued that madness was largely defined by language; it was instituted by particular social communities or nations as an instrument of exclusion, silence and suppression, to be used against insurgent elements. (Writers such as Julia Kristeva, Michel Foucault and R. D. Laing have drawn upon and worked with these ideas.) Artaud answered the language of madness with his poetic language of opposition and furious rejection in *Van Gogh the Suicide of society*. By the end of his life, Artaud was using screams and gestures to refuse and disintegrate any idea, definition or diagnosis of madness.

Artaud continued to travel into Paris from Ivry on most days during the spring of 1947. On 17 March he went to the Sorbonne to hear the former Dada leader, Tristan Tzara, give a lecture on the role of Surrealism after the recent war. Tzara's position was that Surrealism was now obsolete – it had run its course, and the remaining members of the Surrealist movement should turn to Marxism. Much of the audience had come to heckle and then to walk out in protest. Breton stood up and shouted at Tzara, and walked out, followed by Prevel. Artaud left soon afterwards. Also in March, Artaud went to the cinema for the last time in his life. He was walking past the Champollion cinema and saw that Gance's 1935 film *Lucrecia Borgia*, in which he played the role of Savonarola, was being shown. He went inside, but when he saw himself on the screen in a monk's costume, it made him furious. Artaud could not tolerate religion of any kind now. As a counterweight to Breton's Surrealist exhibition, which was to open in July, Artaud was beginning to contemplate an exhibition of his own drawings. His consumption of drugs was at a high level in these months, and he fluctuated between declaring that opium was the most important substance in life, and wretchedly desiring an end to his addiction. Montmartre was the principal area in Paris where drugs could be bought, and Artaud often had to make the journey there. He told Prevel: 'I owe 2,000 francs to one drug-dealer and 5,000 to another. One of them came to see me, the one from Montmartre, but he didn't insist. I told him: "Look, I've only got 20 francs left." With me, he soon realized that it was no good insisting, that I was too far gone when it comes to drugs.'[29] In April, he briefly considered a detoxification cure. Dr Delmas at Ivry was far more understanding than Ferdière had been about Artaud's drug intake; he always treated Artaud kindly, and also allowed him to draw his portrait. Artaud reported to Prevel: 'My testicles suppurated all through the night with a thick, blackish pus. Doctor Delmas said to me: "That's beyond my science", and he added: "You need a gramme of heroin every day."'[30]

Maintaining the momentum of *Van Gogh the Suicide of society*, Artaud produced text after text. In April, he wrote 'Shit to the Mind', attacking all the artistic groupings whose names ended with the suffix 'ism', ranging from Surrealism to the emergent movement of Lettrism. For Artaud, they all made the same grave error in attaching pre-eminence to the mind, or to the spirit, and in subordinating the body. Artaud equated the idea of the mind with the vulnerability of the unconscious and with religious spirituality. The volatile new body he was imagining would abruptly negate the functions of the mind, together with all the mental processes which had caused Artaud himself so much pain. In a long letter of 23 April to Pierre Loeb, Artaud continued to construct this imagery of the autonomous, mind-less body. The body would be powered only by its own intentions, moving as 'a tree of walking will'.[31] It would be stripped down to bone and electric nerve, so as to facilitate the expulsion of its organs. He believed that his individual struggle towards the 'authentic' body rendered the growing Cold War conflict between the United States and the Soviet Union utterly without significance, even if it came to nuclear warfare. During this period, Artaud was also collecting his texts on the Tarahumaras for the publisher Marc Barbezat, and he revised the translation from *Through the Looking Glass* which he had undertaken for Ferdière at Rodez in September 1943.

In May 1947, Artaud's portraits of his friends changed. He began to damage the images more ferociously, and he used coloured crayons as well as pencils to intensify his pictorial assaults on the facial flesh and to reformulate it. He also started to surround his images with texts. They ran around the borders of the drawings, and served to open out what Artaud wanted the face to show, by reinforcing it with a linguistic element. Sometimes the text cut straight across the face, or pushed it into an extreme corner of the drawing's surface space. The written word and the drawn image always generated a strong visual collision. On 22 May Artaud drew a portrait of Paule Thévenin's sister, Minouche Pastier, with sprays of orange, red and blue fire in her hair. Two days later, he drew Paule Thévenin's head surrounded by blocks of metal, her throat gouged and trailing wire, her hair streaming with nails, and her facial skin embedded with a layered arrangement of marks which the passage of a further forty-five years would only begin to give her in life. Artaud also produced two portraits of Colette Thomas, which demonstrate the acute fluctuation of his feelings for her. In the first, her face is delicately formed, with the eyes and the mouth especially emphasized and exposed. In the second portrait, the face is almost unrecognizable; the skin is darkly bruised and slashed by pencil strokes, and the hair falls in tattered bunches around the woman's head. The writing around these drawings of women relate to their status and rivalry as 'daughters of the heart'. On the drawing of Paule Thévenin, Artaud inscribed:

> I put my daughter on guard
> she is faithful
> since Ophelia got up too late

('Ophelia' referred to Colette Thomas, whose mental state was precarious.) Artaud drew a portrait of Prevel's girlfriend Jany de Ruy with the text:

> I make these children
> out of poor wrinkles, and I send them to battle in my body.

Artaud's own face appears in all these portraits, compacted into that of his sitter, so that they are all double portraits of Artaud and the subject whose face he was interrogating in his drawing. Each image is a face-to-face confrontation.

Pierre Loeb offered to mount an exhibition of Artaud's drawings at his Galerie Pierre in the rue des Beaux Arts. Since the exhibition was not intended to make money, Artaud agreed with Loeb that he would forfeit a number of his drawings to the gallery, to offset Loeb's expenses. In the event, more drawings would disappear while they were being hung on the gallery walls or taken down. The drawings which Artaud chose to exhibit were mainly the portraits of the face which he had recently been working on, but a small number of the fragmented figures from his time at Rodez would also be shown. He began to plan two events to mark the opening and closing of the exhibition. During the course of June, he wrote a text entitled *The Human Face* for the exhibition catalogue, which would contain that text alone and no reproductions of Artaud's drawings, because of the expense that would have entailed. He had already written one text on his drawings since he had arrived back in Paris, 'Ten Years that Language has been Gone', in April. It was about the drawings which he used to punctuate his exercise-book fragments, giving their concerns greater immediacy with a dense, gestural illustration. Each of the drawings was 'a machine which is breathing'.[32] Like the physical language of screams and gestures which Artaud was searching for, the drawings would begin with a blow:

> a blow
> anti-logical
> anti-philosophical,
> anti-intellectual,
> anti-*dialectical*
> of language
> pressed down by my black pencil
> and that's all.[33]

The Human Face concentrated on the resuscitation which Artaud intended to give the face, through his wild pencil strokes:

> In fact, the human face carries a kind of perpetual death on its face and it is up to the painter himself to save it with his strokes by giving it back its rightful features.[34]

Artaud had no regard whatsoever for the technical skill and abilities of an artist. He denounced abstract art as an insincere amalgam of technique and money. And he stressed the savagely un-artistic, exploratory nature of his own drawings, which he intended to work at the limits of what could be done with corporeal substances. He wrote:

> I have moreover definitively broken with art, style and talent in all the drawings which you will see here. I mean that I curse anyone who is going to consider them as works of art, works that aes-thetically simulate reality.
> None of them, to speak exactly, is a work. They are all attempts,

that is to say blows – probings or thrustings in all the directions of hazard, of possibility, of chance, or of destiny.[35]

The exhibition of Artaud's drawings at the Galerie Pierre opened on 4 July 1947, in the same month as the International Exhibition of Surrealism at the far larger Galerie Maeght. The event Artaud arranged for the first night did not go well. He had asked Colette Thomas and Marthe Robert to read from his work. Colette Thomas performed a theatre text which Artaud had written in May, entitled *Alienate the Actor*. Artaud's concept of alienation had nothing at all to do with Bertolt Brecht's. Artaud's actor was to be a madman whose life was endangered by society, and who would release his body's force of fury as an act of alienation against that society. Artaud's theatre of the body would be made up from a raw, grinding process of transformation:

> The theatre
> is the condition,
> the place,
> the point,
> where the human anatomy can be seized
> and used to heal and direct life.[36]

Colette Thomas had not rehearsed her reading with Artaud, and she was in a highly strained state at the event. Prevel was present, and described what happened:

> The crowd was dense. I could hardly move, and the heat was overwhelming.
> Colette Thomas was horribly nervous, with an unbearable stage-fright. She began as though she had been thrown into water and never managed to take control of herself for an instant. It was at once pathetic and extremely painful.
> Marthe Robert was more calm and read a text on the Tara-humaras. Artaud, hidden, accentuated the text with savage screams.[37]

Artaud prepared the second Galerie Pierre event with greater discipline. He decided to deliver a text himself, and thereby appear in public for the first time since the Vieux-Colombier performance. But this time he was determined to exert an exact control over what happened. Entrance to the event would be by invitation only, and Artaud would appear surrounded by his own drawings, as though by an army. The performance space would include Artaud's visual, aural and physical presence. The text he wrote for his performance was entitled *The Theatre and science*. The only science Artaud would recognize as valid was one which formulated a physical gesture that could annihilate death, society and the organs of the body, to create a body in constant movement. 'Theatre' was the name which Artaud gave to this all-consuming action:

> The true theatre has always appeared to me as the exercise of a dangerous, terrible action,
> where the idea of theatre and of spectacle are eliminated
> together with those of all science, all religion and all art.
> The action I am talking about aims for the organic transformation and the authentic physicality of the human body.
> Why?
> Because the theatre . . . is this crucible of fire and real meat where, anatomically,
> by stampings of bones, limbs and syllables, bodies are remade.[38]

Artaud wrote to Roger Blin asking him to perform at the second event, and he harassed Colette Thomas into intensively rehearsing her second reading of *Alienate the Actor* with him at Ivry. On 5 July, she complained to Prevel that 'I have no money, and Artaud tries to kiss me. I don't know what is going to happen.'[39]

The second Galerie Pierre event took place on 18 July, two days before the end of Artaud's exhibition. According to one of the audience, Claire Goll, Ferdière was present and was 'almost lynched'.[40] Prevel was there and documented the performances:

> There were lots of people. It was stifling.
> Artaud spoke first, with a great rigour of meaning, his voice was clear, and his command was total. Absolutely the opposite of his lecture.[41]
> Then Colette Thomas – extraordinary – and as Artaud expressed it: 'Like a mind ready to materialize.'
> Roger Blin read *The Indian Culture* in a phenomenal way and lifted the audience off the ground.
> 'Roger Blin was like a devil,' Artaud said.[42]

Between Colette Thomas's reading and that of Roger Blin, Marthe Robert again performed *The Tarahumaras' Peyote Rite*, as she had done on 4 July. Since then Artaud had found a gong, which he beat with a huge poker to punctuate the words Marthe Robert was reading. The event was a great success. But for Artaud, it had still not generated all the impact which he wanted his language to

create. On the same evening, he wrote a postscript to his manuscript of *The Theatre and science*:

> This reading took place this evening, Friday 18 July 1947, and by
> moments it was as though I *skimmed the opening* of my heart's tone.
> I would have had to *shit* blood through my navel to arrive at what I
> want.
> For example, three quarters of an hour's beating with a poker on
> the same spot . . .[43]

Two days later, he told Prevel that 'in spite of everything I was
disappointed. I believe that in order to make all these people
understand something, I would have to kill them.'[44] Artaud continued to be confident that he would soon reach the level of direct
action which he had formulated in *The Theatre and science*, and had
attempted to put into practice with the Galerie Pierre event. But he
still needed to bring that action into existence, and drive it through
to its extreme end. He continued to make many drawings in the
weeks after the exhibition. He believed that it would be through the
intermediary of his visual images that the violent welding of language with the body could be achieved. On 21 August, he wrote to
Marc Barbezat:

> I have the idea of putting into operation a new gathering-together
> of the human world's activities, idea of a new *anatomy*.
> My drawings are *anatomies* in action.[45]

From the time of his exhibition, Artaud's health began to decline
rapidly. He complained of pains all over his body, his face became
swollen and he had to spend days incapacitated in his bed at Ivry.
His journeys into Paris became rarer in the autumn of 1947, but
Artaud's physical suffering never stopped him working. He continued to write texts, draw, dance, and hammer at the wooden
block in his pavilion, working to drive his pain away. Now that
Artaud was less visible in Saint Germain-des-Prés, he had greater
difficulty in arranging meetings with his friends, and he began to
feel isolated at Ivry. Paule Thévenin went to visit him regularly –
she had been away in Morocco during the exhibition – and a young
unemployed actor named André Voisin began appearing each
morning at Ivry, helping Artaud with the everyday business of his
life which was becoming increasingly impossible for him. He also
saw Colette Thomas often, but he was estranging her with his
behaviour and demands. He declared that she believed she had

written Artaud's texts herself, and that he had stolen them from her. He also complained that she wanted to seduce him and have a baby by him.

Finding it difficult to obtain laudanum regularly under the black market conditions, Artaud began to take enormous doses of chloral hydrate, which he swallowed in the form of a syrup. Chloral hydrate is an addictive, hypnotic drug, rarely used in medical practice to kill pain; it has many side-effects, notably as a gastric irritant, and its function is to put the patient to sleep rapidly. Artaud found it hard to regulate his dose, and often fell into comas. When he did go into Paris, he often collapsed in the street. In August, three policemen picked him up and took him back to the clinic in a taxi. On one occasion at the beginning of November, he blacked out in the place Blanche in Montmartre, and awoke to find that the fifteen thousand francs he had been carrying had disappeared. Prevel spent much of his time searching for laudanum to take to Ivry. But on the night of 11 August, Prevel had his first serious tubercular haemorrhage and became gravely ill. Two days later, Artaud wrote to him:

> I waited for you
> all day yesterday.
> Come to Ivry
> anyway
> I cannot MOVE
> from here in the
> horrible
> state I am in
> I am waiting for you.[46]

Prevel kept desperately trying to find laudanum for Artaud, but on 4 September he had to be hospitalized. Even so, Artaud's demands continued; he made several visits to the hospital, but Prevel could now do nothing. Although he was to survive Artaud by three years, his life as a poet and as Artaud's companion was over. In October, to Artaud's sadness, Dr Delmas died. Artaud considered that Delmas was the only doctor who had ever done him any good. Delmas's successor, Dr Rallu, was far less understanding about Artaud's addiction than Delmas had been. Artaud began to consider leaving the clinic and moving to Provence, where he hoped to be able to recover his health. Towards the end of October, Artaud was so ill that he was told he should be transferred to a clinic at Le

Vésinet in the western suburbs of Paris, before travelling south. But he stubbornly stayed in his Ivry pavilion.

Artaud's writings were now crammed with invective and denunciation. In November, he wrote several texts with the same title, 'I Hate and Expel', in which he rhythmically condemned a huge range of people, and ejected them from his world: 'I hate and expel as cowardly all beings who do not recognize that life is given to them only so that they can entirely remake and reconstitute their bodies . . .'[47] For Artaud, everything he needed to survive, everything that would have made up a world he could have lived in, had still to be created:

> We are not yet born,
> we are not yet in the world,
> there is not yet a world,
> things have not yet been made,
> the reason for being has not yet been found.[48]

In the last part of his life Artaud often wrote to the newspaper *Combat*, demanding a massive readership for his individual concerns. In one letter to Albert Camus at *Combat*, he wrote: 'The erotic sexual life of France is sombre, Mr Albert Camus, it is black like its market.'[49] On 1 November, for the only time, *Combat* published one of Artaud's letters, in the wake of a literary quarrel over whether a current production by Jean Vilar of Shakespeare's *Richard II* had adopted Artaud's proposals in *The Theatre and its Double*. *Combat* had already published an extract from *Van Gogh the Suicide of society* on 2 May. Artaud's letter appeared next to a cartoon of him wearing a beret and angrily shaking his fist, and was titled '"For thirty years I've had something vital to say," Antonin Artaud writes to us.' In the letter, Artaud looked back over all his time as a writer, to the Rivière correspondence, the early Surrealist poetry, and *The Theatre and its Double*. The vital thing had never been expressed because Artaud's language had always betrayed him, as had his readership. He now reacted against that failure by declaring that 'it is the very reason for being of language and grammar that I unhinge'.[50] Then he inserted some of his invented language into the context of the mass-circulation newspaper, and made an appeal for the creation of a resistant new body which would obliterate his enemies.

In the first days of November, immediately after the publication of his letter in *Combat*, Artaud received an invitation which he believed would enable him to reach an even wider audience. The invitation came from Fernand Pouey, head of dramatic and literary broadcasts at the French national radio station. He wanted Artaud to record a long broadcast on whatever subject he desired. Artaud could choose his own collaborators and have as much rehearsal time as he needed. The broadcast would be for a series of programmes entitled *The Voice of the Poets* which Pouey was preparing, and would be transmitted on the Parisian channel. Artaud immediately accepted. The recording would have a far greater scope and potential impact than those he had done in June and July 1946 for *Club d'Essai*. It would give him the opportunity to develop some notes he had been making in September and October towards a performance on the theme of 'the last judgement'. For Artaud, the idea of divine judgement had to be disintegrated, so that he could determine his own final movements and his own apocalypse. His initial idea for the recording was that it would comprise of:

> Exclamations,
> interjections, screams,
> interruptions, interrogations
> on
> the putting into question
> of
> the Last Judgement.[51]

He decided on the title *To have done with the judgement of god*. In his last years, Artaud invariably wrote 'god' rather than 'God', as an expression of his contempt for all religions (particularly the Christian faith), and for what he viewed as their cowardly subjugation of the self to a fabricated divinity.

When Artaud began to choose material for the recording, his concept escalated to include all his crucial concerns – cries and gestures, psychiatry and madness, the Tarahumaras, language and the new body. In October, he had written a new text on the Tarahumaras' peyote dance for Marc Barbezat, and decided to include that. He urgently wrote a number of new texts before the recording sessions, including one entitled 'The Theatre of Cruelty', which could not be used in the broadcast because of time constraints. In this text, Artaud pointed to the origins of disease and death in the absence of an authentic theatre, which he would create as an amalgamation of violent dances and cries. He formulated his new Theatre of Cruelty as one of 'furious revolt/from the destitution of the human body'.[52] Artaud was making notes all through the period leading up to the recording sessions, deciding how he wanted his recorded language to operate. His principal desire was to cancel out the entire process of mediation and signification. He wanted his work to be immediately and physically experienced. He believed this would be possible, through the unique force of his material and its delivery. The hostility which Artaud had felt for representation and repetition in the early 1930s had now developed to its most acute point. He conceived of representation as a malicious instrument of social suppression:

> There is nothing I abominate and shit upon so much as this idea of representation,
>> that is, of virtuality, of non-reality,
>> attached to all that is produced and shown,
>> . . . as if it were intended in this way to socialize and at the same time paralyse monsters, make the possibilities of explosive deflagration which are too dangerous for life pass instead by the channel of the stage, the screen or the microphone, and so turn them away from life.[53]

What Artaud was planning for the transmission of his work would resist this process to an extreme degree:

> I abject all signs.
> I create only machines of instant utility.[54]

Artaud asked Roger Blin, Paule Thévenin and Colette Thomas to read from his work for the recording. Blin said he would find Artaud the best radio producer in Paris. Artaud refused, saying he wanted the worst. That way, he should meet with little interference. Paule Thévenin was the only one of the four participants who had no professional acting experience, although Artaud had already worked with her, teaching her how she should scream until her breath was exhausted. He allowed her to choose for herself what she would read, and she decided on a text from one of Artaud's exercise-books from October 1947. There was only one reading under Artaud's supervision, and no rehearsal, before the recording sessions. Artaud let all his collaborators find their own rhythms and intonations for the texts they were reading, before giving them one or two instructions each. Shortly before the recording sessions started, Colette Thomas abruptly refused to participate; Artaud

said this was due to a 'caprice'[55] on her part. A replacement to read
the Tarahumaras text had to be found quickly. Artaud wanted it to
be a woman, so that his recording would have two male and two
female voices. Paule Thévenin asked the young Spanish actress
Maria Casarès, who had read a text by Artaud at the benefit
performance on 7 June 1946, if she would take Colette Thomas's
place. Casarès was becoming increasingly renowned, and the
following month she would appear in the hugely successful first
production of Henri Pichette's *The Epiphanies*, along with Gérard
Philippe and Roger Blin. She went on to play the Princess of Death
in Jean Cocteau's film *Orpheus*, and would appear in the celebrated
production of Jean Genet's *The Screens* directed by Roger Blin at
the Odéon theatre in Paris in 1966. At the time of the recording of
To have done with the judgement of god, Casarès was in 'a state of
aggravated euphoria which kept me upright, hardly sleeping, for
seven whole weeks, at the borders of reality, and which carried me
when I did sleep into arid, devastated regions, where nightmares of
futurist warfare mixed together the most refined weapons and
means ever invented to pursue solitary fugitives.'[56]

With his collaborators, Artaud recorded all the texts for his
broadcast between 22 and 29 November 1947. A further recording
session was held on 16 January 1948, at which Artaud performed
long screams, cries, and percussive beatings. These passages of
noise were to be interspersed between the spoken texts. Roger Blin
was present at the recording session of 16 January, and he and
Artaud performed a dialogue in Artaud's invented language.
Artaud called this dialogue 'the monkeys' cage'. These creations of
noise were extremely important to Artaud. He intended them to
fracture the process of representation, cutting across his spoken
texts just as the drawings did with the texts in his exercise-books,
intensifying his concerns with a gestural eruption. On the same
day, 16 January, Artaud heard a rough montage of the recording
assembled by Fernand Pouey and the radio producer, René Guig-
nard. Artaud instructed Pouey to cut part of the spoken text he had
recorded for the beginning of the broadcast, so that the noise-
effects would be more prominent; he also re-recorded the broadcast's final text. Pouey disregarded both Artaud's requested cut,
and his re-recording. The date of the transmission was set for 2
February 1948, at 10.45 in the evening. Artaud was satisfied with
his recording, and expected it to cause a huge uproar when it was
transmitted. He declared that he was happy his work would finally

reach people like roadmenders, whom he regarded highly because they were were engaged in hard and unrelentingly physical work; this was how he conceived of his own work.

To have done with the judgement of god has five parts, intercut with Artaud's noise-effects. The first long section is performed by Artaud himself, and deals with an imagined American government practice of stockpiling schoolboys' sperm to provide soldiers for the financially motivated wars of the future. Artaud's voice tears at the words, with cold humour. The second section, 'Tutuguri, the Rite of the Black Sun', is read by Casarès, and concerns Artaud's 1947 interpretation of the Tarahumaras' dance. He now saw the dance as specifically abolishing the Christian cross; a new sign was then forged from bleeding flesh and fire. 'The Search for the Excremental' is performed by Roger Blin, and states Artaud's opposition of bone to excrement. The text taunts men for having cowardly bodies of meat and excrement when

> to live,
> you have to be somebody,
> to be somebody,
> you have to have a BONE,
> and not be afraid of showing the bone,
> and losing the meat in the process.[57]

Artaud asserts that an army has now revolted to end the judgement of 'god' by creating a body totally without organs, such as Artaud yearned for. The fourth text, 'The Question Arises', read by Paule Thévenin, attacks the mythical status accorded to ideas in language; for Artaud, ideas are the waste products and the internal gasses of the body. He counterposes them with his belief in 'infinity', which he sees as

> the opening
> of our consciousness
> towards possibility
> beyond measure.[58]

Artaud performs the recording's closing text. He interrupts himself in the voice of the listening public, who demand that he be silenced and put in a strait-jacket. In reaction, Artaud pleads more and more desperately for the remaking of the human body on an autopsy table, and for a painful scraping-away of 'god' and the internal organs. Finally, he calls for the creation of a delirious but disciplined wrong-way-round dance of the body.

To have done with the judgement of god is an enormously ambitious and innovative project. Artaud constructed an intricate arrangement for his screams, silences and spoken texts. The recording was arranged 'at a hairsbreadth/in a fulminating order'.[59] His screams are the dark core of the recording, and suck in all the other elements. Artaud intended his work to make the body be felt in all its extremity. The recorded sound itself had to have a physical presence in space, and as it was spat out had to re-create itself constantly as a set of scars inflicted upon the exterior world. Artaud's aim was not to tell a story or produce any kind of illusion. Voices are layered behind voices in a dense trajectory of sound which acts and moves in a multiplicity of directions. His scream, executed in a swarm of chance and disciplined events, is an overwhelming rush of vocal sound. It demonstrates the extraordinary regaining of Artaud's voice after the imposed silence and physical restraint of his long asylum internment. With this seized-back voice, Artaud tries to disrupt the structures of language, to fracture them irreparably, so that the physical life which they screen can emerge.

Artaud closely involved laughter in his language. *To have done with the judgement of god* is a ferociously funny piece of work. Artaud's laughter is an explosive attack and taunting. He ridicules the diagnoses and definitions of insanity applied to him by the asylum doctors, and adeptly turns the concept of madness back upon psychiatric medicine. His laughter is also outrage, a contemptuous probing of what he saw as the flawed human body. More deeply, Artaud's laughter is a violent exploration of sense, and of the known and repeatable – and therefore, for Artaud, socially containable and assimilable – aspects of language. Artaud reveals what is hidden by that language: the heterogeneous, many-tongued human body. His struggle is one of endurance. He writes that his work

> is not the symbol of an absent void,
> of an appalling incapacity of people to realize themselves in life.
> It is the affirmation
> of a terrible
> and moreover inescapable necessity.[60]

In *To have done with the judgement of god*, Artaud aims to reach the body directly, to establish an existence for the body in which all influence, all nature and all culture are torn away, so that the body is by itself, honed to bone and nerve, as pure intention, without family, society or religion. Artaud's language in *To have done with the judgement of god* is itself reduced and sharpened to express his need to cut into, destroy and reformulate the body; at times, everything bursts in upon the ear at once. Artaud's language is fragmented; simultaneously, the desire it carries for physical transmission and transformation sutures the pieces together again in the listener.

The writing and recording of *To have done with the judgement of god* exhausted Artaud, and used up his remaining strength. He rarely left Ivry now; when he went to visit Paule Thévenin in Charenton, a car was sent to pick him up. He was still thinking of leaving the clinic, and wrote to Marc Barbezat on 15 December: 'I am going to undertake a great journey to the South, have a change of climate, remake my health which is injured, damaged . . .'[61] The general pain he had experienced in the autumn had now localized in his abdomen. His complaints about the organs of his body grew in bitterness. He continued to write extensively during December 1947 and January 1948, but his work now consisted almost entirely of fragments. He gave many of them to the young writer Marcel Bisiaux, for his magazine *84* (Bisiaux lived at number 84 in the rue Saint Louis en l'Île). Artaud's fragments were abrupt gestural expulsions:

> It's very cold
> as when
> it's
> Artaud the dead man
> who
> breathes.[62]

They articulated his feeling of being torn between his forceful denial of death – which was becoming eroded as he realized he was dangerously ill – and his belief that when he died, his body would explode into flames and into fragments of multiple new bodies.

Artaud drew until the very end of his life. In the drawings from his last months, the faces became progressively more autopsied. They carried a sense of death, which was ground deeper and deeper into their substance. But the transformed bones and eyes were also infused with life. The final drawings were accumulations of heads, piled up on top of each other as totems. The face of Artaud appeared both as a handsome young man and as a prematurely dying and toothless fifty-year-old man. His own faces were surrounded by those of people from his past life who had died, such as Yvonne Allendy, and people from his immediate life, such as Paule Thévenin. In a self-portrait which he dated December 1948 (and which appears as a continuing refusal of death, since he would not live that long), Artaud's head was drawn like a skull composed of the hardest bone. His twisted and erect hand dominated the image, and an oppressive death's-head was fixed at his shoulder as a double of his own head. The idea of the double still had a crucial presence in Artaud's work. The double was what threatened to kill him, but it could also serve to resuscitate his life. One of Artaud's last completed drawings, made in December 1947 to January 1948, was entitled *The Projection of the True Body*. It showed Artaud's own body being shot by a firing-squad, his hands chained and his kneecaps heavily scored-through, while opposite stood his double, a black skeleton with its life wildly spurting outward around its bones in torrential lines of force. The two bodies were bound together.

At the end of January 1948, Artaud decided to assemble a book of the drawings from his exercise-books, and asked Paule Thévenin to choose the fifty she found most beautiful. Pierre Loeb was to have been the book's publisher. On 31 January Artaud produced a text, *50 Drawings to Assassinate Magic*, to accompany the book. He wrote that his drawings

> will make their apocalypse
> because they have said too much to be born
> and said too much in being born
> not to be reborn
> and take a body
> and so authentically.[63]

The project went no further.

In the months of December 1947 and January 1948, three of the projects undertaken by Artaud since his return to Paris were published in rapid succession. *Artaud the Mômo* was published by Bordas on 15 December, and *Van Gogh the Suicide of society* appeared at the same time with the publisher K, in a relatively large and inexpensive edition of three thousand copies; around 20 January, K also published *Here Lies preceded by The Indian Culture*. These books increased the anticipation in Paris for Artaud's broadcast, scheduled for 2 February. On 16 January, Artaud was in the recording studio performing the screams for his broadcast. Just as he completed an immensely long and devastating scream, the writer Raymond

Queneau came into the studio to tell him that he had won his first ever literary prize, the modest Prix Sainte-Beuve for best essay of 1947, awarded to *Van Gogh the Suicide of society*.

By this time, Artaud was suffering severe intestinal pain and haemorrhages, and he had grown emaciated. He complained frequently of 'the beast eating into his anus'.[64] Paule Thévenin's husband Yves was an obstetrician, and persuaded Artaud to consult a gastro-enterologist. Artaud's horror of the medical profession made him resistant to the idea, but he relented and the consultation took place on 19 January. The gastro-enterologist suspected a serious problem, and recommended that Artaud consult the renowned specialist Henri Mondor at the Salpêtrière hospital in Paris. An appointment was set for 27 January. The journey to the south of France was now arranged. Artaud would move out of his pavilion on 15 March, and travel with Paule Thévenin to Antibes, where a villa had been rented for him. At the first consultation at the Salpêtrière, X-rays were taken and Artaud agreed to go back on 3 February to hear Mondor's diagnosis.

On the afternoon of 1 February, the day before Artaud's recording *To have done with the judgement of god* was due to be transmitted, the head of the radio station Wladimir Porché listened to the work and immediately banned it. The grounds he gave were that it was inflammatory, obscene and blasphemous. Paule Thévenin has said that the censorship imposed upon Artaud's recording was executed with arbitrary disdain and abruptness, 'just as though it were a porno movie'.[65] Artaud was deeply wounded and angry. The denial of a mass audience for his work particularly incensed him. He wrote a letter to Porché, declaring that the people of Paris had been hoping for 'deliverance'[66] in the form of his recording. Fernand Pouey was also outraged, and threatened to resign. (He would face a similar situation of being overruled after he had commissioned Jean Genet's projected broadcast, *The Criminal Child*.) A press scandal ensued about the ban, with the newspapers divided over whether Artaud's work should be transmitted. In *Combat*, the journalist René Guilly discussed 'the case of Artaud' in literary terms, and recommended that he should stick to writing books. Artaud replied:

THE DUTY
   of the writer, of the poet
   is not to cowardly shut himself away in a text, a book, a magazine,
from which he will never emerge

> but on the contrary to emerge
> go outside
> to shake
> to attack
> the mind of the public
> if not
> what use is he?[67]

Fernand Pouey organized two private auditions of the recording, hoping that he would accumulate enough support to overturn Porché's ruling. At the first event, on 5 February, a prestigious audience including Jean Cocteau, Paul Éluard and a Dominican priest named Laval listened to Artaud's recording in a studio at the radio station. They unanimously agreed with Pouey that it should be transmitted. Artaud strongly resented the approval of the priest (who would subsequently give the last rites to Génica Athanasiou's lover, Jean Grémillon), and wrote him a furious letter of repudiation. Porché ignored the audience's approval of the recording, and Artaud knew the ban would not be lifted. He rapidly agreed to have the recording's texts published as a book, but the silencing of his screams, cries and beatings was a terrible blow. He wrote to Jean Paulhan:

> the sounds will not be heard,
> the resounding xylophony,
> the screams, the guttural noises and the voice,
>   all of which would have at last constituted a first grinding-over of
> the Theatre of Cruelty.
> This is a DISASTER for me.[68]

The second audition of the recording took place at a disused cinema. (Its name, 'The Washington', was the same as that of the boat on which Artaud had been placed in a strait-jacket in 1937.) The event was reserved principally for the working people Artaud had come into contact with at Ivry, including his barber and tobacconist. Arthur Adamov and Marthe Robert attended the event, and made criticisms of Artaud's recording which upset him still further. For many years, the recording of *To have done with the judgement of god* was known only from a few clandestine copies belonging to Artaud's collaborators and friends.

On 3 February, the day after he had written his letter of protest to Porché, Artaud returned to the Salpêtrière with Paule Thévenin to hear Mondor's diagnosis. It was reassuring: Mondor prescribed a treatment and told Artaud to stay in bed for several months. But, out of Artaud's earshot, Mondor told Paule Thévenin that Artaud had a long-standing and inoperable intestinal cancer. He wrote a letter for Dr Rallu at the Ivry clinic, authorizing Artaud to have what he had wanted for so many years – an unrestricted access to laudanum. That was all that might kill his pain. Although Paule Thévenin did not tell him that he had cancer, Artaud knew it. Mondor's diagnosis implied that Artaud's cancer had been developing during his time at Rodez. Gaston Ferdière has defended himself against the fact that he did not detect the disease there. He wrote that 'the diagnosis of intestinal cancer which one fine day fell from the mouth of Professor Henri Mondor appears to me to be subject to caution',[69] and argued that, in looking at the X-rays, Mondor might have mistaken the residue of opium in Artaud's intestines for opaque cancerous formations.

Artaud continued to write through his last weeks, attempting to strengthen his failing body with a battered and scarred carapace of language. In one fragment from February 1948, he met his oncoming death as a confrontation and final resolution of physical substance with fire:

> Make the human body emerge
> into the light of nature
> plunge it raw into the glow of nature
> where the sun will finally embrace with it.[70]

Artaud still made occasional journeys into Paris, and on 13 February he went to see the publisher Pierre Bordas in Montparnasse. Bordas's secretary refused to let Artaud see him, which made Artaud furious. He wrote to Bordas on the following day, instructing him to cease publishing his books. Artaud accused Bordas of cheating him over his work: 'You have made a killing with *Artaud the Mômo*, picked up a fortune, all that stinks.'[71] (Bordas, who had issued Artaud's book in an edition of only 355 copies, started specializing in textbook publishing soon after this.) Since Artaud had arranged for 'Tutuguri, the Rite of the Black Sun' to be published in the collection of texts recorded for *To have done with the judgement of god*, on 16 February he wrote a new text about the peyote dance, entitled 'Tutuguri', for the book on the Tarahumaras which Marc Barbezat was preparing to publish. The text was closely allied to the atmosphere of *To have done with the judgement of god*. Artaud's final interpretation of the peyote dance saw it as causing the absolute destruction and death of the sun in an explosion of bleeding bodies, immense flames, and ferocious caco-phonies:

> At the borders of the noise and the void – since the noise is so strong
> that it calls
> before it
> only the void,
> there is then an immense stamping.[72]

On the same day that he wrote 'Tutuguri', Artaud sent it to Marc Barbezat. In the accompanying letter, he described the origin of his text in his desperately ill body:

> The new *Tutuguri* which I am sending you is heavy with a blood-soaked experience which I did not have in 1936.
> This blood-soaked experience is that I have just had 3 attacks here and was found *swimming* in my blood,
> a whole pool of blood and the *Tutuguri* I enclose comes out of that . . .[73]

Despite his awareness of his imminent death, Artaud still antici-pated that the journey to Antibes with Paule Thévenin would take place, and asked Barbezat to send him money to cover the costs of the move. On 23 February, Artaud had dinner with Paule Thé-venin in a Parisian restaurant; he felt he could 'no longer eat without spitting'.[74] He was still wounded by the censorship of *To have done with the judgement of god*, but was now planning a new stage of his work, more virulent and dangerous than ever –

> a theatre of blood,
> a theatre where at each performance
> something
> will be won
> *physically* . . .
> In reality, the theatre is the *birth* of creation.
> That will happen.[75]

In the final week of his life, Artaud gave two newspaper inter-views in the wake of the furore over his recording. (They were his first interviews since those about the production of *The Cenci* in 1935.) The first interview, in the last days of February, was with Jean Marabini from *Combat*. Artaud made it clear that he was fully conscious of his grave physical state: 'I know I have cancer. What I want to say before dying is that I hate psychiatrists.'[76] He was still denying death, but not his own. He evoked a time in the past when people in isolated places of the world were immortal. Despite the agonies of his body, Artaud was still concerned to give the anatomy predominance in his language. He described the gestural immediacy and vitality of a seizing hand which could cut away mental processes from the body. As Artaud moved towards death, he was more than ever concerned to obliterate the mental: 'At this moment, I want to destroy my thought and my mind. Above all, thought, mind and consciousness. I do not want to suppose anything, admit anything, enter into anything, discuss anything . . .'[77] Shortly afterwards, on 28 February, Artaud gave his last interview, to Jean Desternes from *Le Figaro Littéraire*. The necessity of denouncing psychiatry and electroshock was still crucial for Artaud, and he described again his experience of death in the Rodez electroshock coma: 'Yes, I saw the hideous face of death . . . I plunged into death. I know what death is.'[78] He also recalled his journey to Ireland and the attack in Dublin during which he was struck with an iron bar: 'And it was on that day that the terrible tortures started, which – according to psychiatrists – are the result of hallucinations.'[79] The intention which Artaud always had to direct his creative language away from the frailties of words, towards cruelty and gestural explosivity, was finally becoming crushed: 'I have been haunted for so long, *haun-ted* by a kind of writing which is not in the norm. I would like to write outside of grammar, find a means of expression beyond words. And I occasionally believe that I am very close to that expression . . . but everything pulls me back to the norm.'[80]

Artaud's sister, Marie-Ange, visited him on the afternoon of Tuesday, 2 March. The following day he went to see Paule Thévenin at Charenton, and surprised her by drawing up a testament on official paper, entrusting her with the publication of his books. He had recently been declaring that he would no longer write, that he had written everything, and had finished. But he kept on writing, to the last days of his life. His final fragment views his impending death as a hard and finally lost combat, and as a social, religious and sexual swallowing:

> And they have pushed me over
> into death,
> there where I ceaselessly eat
> cock

anus
and caca
at all my meals,
all those of THE CROSS.[81]

He left Paule Thévenin's house in the afternoon, and returned to Ivry. The weather was very cold, with spring snow on the ground. Artaud died at dawn on the following day, 4 March 1948, alone in his pavilion, seated at the foot of his bed, holding his shoe. Arthur Adamov wrote: 'Suicide of Antonin Artaud, by chloral (the massive weapon).'[82] Artaud had been taking great amounts of chloral in the last weeks of his life, but it is by no means certain that he purposely took a lethal dose; the toxic levels of chloral can vary enormously. Certainly, Artaud felt he had accomplished all he could, and his work had now been safely entrusted. Paule Thévenin believed that Artaud died how and probably when he wanted. His body did not burst into unforgettable fragments at death, but his work did.

The gardener at the clinic found Artaud's body when he brought his breakfast in the morning, and the boilerman went to the Ivry town hall to announce that Artaud had died. His friends and family began arriving at the pavilion. Jean Paulhan placed a tiny bouquet of violets between Artaud's fingers, and had a death-mask made of his face. A four-day vigil started, to keep rats away. Artaud's family wanted him to have a Catholic burial service, but Paulhan told the priest that there was a possibility of suicide, thereby ensuring that Artaud would have a civil burial. A substantial part of the money raised for Artaud at the time of his release from Rodez was left unspent, and Paulhan arranged for it to be divided between those of Artaud's friends who most needed it. Of Artaud's closest companions, Jacques Prevel died of tuberculosis in 1951, Arthur Adamov committed suicide in 1970, and Roger Blin died in 1984 after surviving open-heart surgery. Paule Thévenin began the immense project of editing Artaud's *Collected Works*.

Artaud's body was placed in his coffin only at the very last moment. On the morning of 8 March, the funeral procession set out from his pavilion. In later years, the pavilion and clinic would be demolished, and the site used for the construction of suburban blocks of flats. The brief burial service took place at the communal cemetery in Ivry. Artaud's body remained there until 1975, when his family arranged for it to be transferred to the plot which his mother had bought in 1925 for his father, at the Saint Pierre cemetery in Marseilles, not far from the street where Artaud was born. His body now lies there under a large stone cross, in a new tomb with the sole inscription: 'Family of Antonin Artaud'.

As Artaud himself wrote, he was a man who said what he had seen and what he believed. He propelled his visions and beliefs on, to discover their extreme points, until he was immersed by hallucinations, obsessions and catastrophes. But he continued to work, and continued to see. His life ended in wild and raw obliteration, just as he had always wanted. The testing of Artaud's existence – in the form of journeys, writings and images – became his creation. Artaud's life and work move straight to the burning facts of existence and creativity: the body, the gesture, death, sexuality, and language.

Notes

CW = *Collected Works* (*Oeuvres complètes*), Gallimard, Paris, 1956– ; revised edition 1976– , edited by Paule Thévenin.

Introduction

1. Koseki, *L'Autre Journal*, Paris, 26 March 1986, p.55.
2. Collected in Derrida, *L'Écriture et la différence*, Seuil, Paris, 1967; an English translation is collected in *Writing and Difference*, Routledge, London, 1978.
3. *Antonin Artaud, Dessins et portraits* (ed. Paule Thévenin), Gallimard, Paris, 1986.
4. Collected in Kristeva, *Polylogue*, Seuil, Paris, 1977.
5. Lettrisme, Paris, 1970, p.141.
6. Blin, *Souvenirs et propos*, Gallimard, Paris, 1986, p.32.
7. Lacan, 'Raison d'un échec' (1967) in *Scilicet* no. 1, Paris, 1968, p.50.
8. Prevel, *En Compagnie d'Antonin Artaud*, Flammarion, Paris, 1974, p.36.
9. CW VII, 1982, p.309.

Chapter 1: Surrealism and the Void

1. Letter to Jean Paulhan, CW VII, 1982, p.178.
2. *The Theatre of Cruelty* (1947), CW XIII, 1974, p.118.
3. CW XV, 1981, p.164.
4. *Lettres à Génica Athanasiou*, Gallimard, Paris, 1969, p.116.
5. Ibid, p.276.
6. Ibid, p.310.
7. CW I*, 1976, p.40.
8. Ibid, p.41.
9. Ibid, pp.9–10.
10. Ibid, p.10.
11. CW VIII, 1980, p.146.
12. CW I*, p.112.
13. Breton, *Entretiens 1913–1952*, Gallimard, Paris, 1952, p.109.
14. CW I**, 1976, p.20.
15. Ibid, p.41.
16. Ibid, p.221.
17. CW I*, p.18.
18. CW XII, 1974, p.230.
19. 'Shit to the Mind' in *Tel Quel* no. 3, Paris, 1960, p.7.
20. CW I*, p.58.

21. Ibid, p.71.
22. Ibid, p.117.
23. Ibid, p.120.
24. CW II, 1973, p.30.
25. *L'Éphémère* no. 8, Paris, 1968, p.13.
26. 'In Broad Night or the Surrealist Bluff', CW I**, p.60.
27. 'Full Stop', ibid, p.72.
28. CW VII, p.326.
29. Ibid, p.332.
30. 'In Broad Night or the Surrealist Bluff', CW I**, p.60.
31. CW I**, p.67.
32. Ibid, p.74.
33. 'Cinema and Reality', CW III, 1978, p.19.
34. Both the Studio 28 and the Ursulines still operate as repertory cinemas.
35. CW III, p.377.
36. Ibid, p.54.
37. Letter to Jean Paulhan, ibid, p.261.
38. Letter to Louis Jouvet, ibid, p.283.
39. 'Cinema and Reality', CW III, p.19.
40. Ibid, p.20.
41. Ibid, p.20.
42. 'Witchcraft and Cinema', ibid, p.66.
43. 'The Alfred Jarry Theatre: 1928 Season', CW II, p.34.
44. Ibid, p.39.
45. 'The Alfred Jarry Theatre', ibid, p.48.
46. 'The Alfred Jarry Theatre: 1928 Season', ibid, p.38.
47. 'The Alfred Jarry Theatre in 1930', ibid, p.62.
48. 'The Alfred Jarry Theatre: 1928 Season', ibid, p.38.

Chapter 2: The Theatre of Cruelty

1. 'The Theatre and Poetry', CW V, 1979, p.13.
2. 'On the Balinese Theatre', CW IV, 1978, p.50.
3. Ibid, p.57.
4. Grotowski, *Towards a Poor Theatre*, Methuen, London, 1969, p.121.
5. CW IV, p.39.
6. Ibid, p.40.
7. Ibid, p.9.
8. 'Letter to *L'Intransigeant*', CW V, p.27.
9. 'The Marx Brothers', CW IV, p.133.
10. Ibid, p.135.
11. 'The Theatre which I am going to found', CW V, pp.28–9.
12. Letter to Jean Paulhan, CW III, p.259.
13. CW III, p.268.
14. CW II, p.191.
15. Letter to Dr and Mme Allendy, CW I**, p.198.
16. Letter to Jean Paulhan, CW V, p.101.
17. 'The Theatre of Cruelty' (1935 interview), CW V, p.220.

18. CW IV, p.98.
19. Ibid, p.98.
20. CW V, pp.33–4.
21. CW IV, pp.86–7.
22. Ibid, p.88.
23. Ibid, pp.90–1.
24. Ibid, p.91.
25. Ibid, p.92.
26. Ibid, p.93.
27. Ibid, p.95.
28. CW II, p.107.
29. Ibid, p.119.
30. Ibid, p.108.
31. 'Hospitalization of December 1932', CW VIII, 1980, p.320.
32. Ibid, p.322.
33. Letter to André Rolland de Renéville, CW V, p.133.
34. CW V, p.120.
35. Ibid, p.18.
36. Ibid, p.19.
37. CW VII, p.364.
38. *Lettres à Anie Besnard*, Le Nouveau Commerce, Paris, 1977, p.41.
39. *The Journals of Anaïs Nin, 1931–1934* Peter Owen, London, 1966, p.187.
40. Blin, *Souvenirs et propos*, p.32.
41. CW VII, p.279.
42. Ibid, p.13.
43. Ibid, p.18.
44. Ibid, pp.84–5.
45. Ibid, p.110.
46. CW VII, p.153.
47. *The Journals of Anaïs Nin, 1931–1934*, p.229.
48. CW IV, p.27.
49. Ibid, p.31.
50. *The Journals of Anaïs Nin, 1931–1934*, p.192.
51. Letter to André Rolland de Renéville, CW V, p.142.
52. *The Journals of Anaïs Nin, 1931–1934*, p.229.
53. Anaïs Nin, *Je suis le plus malade des surréalistes* in *Under a Glass Bell*, Penguin, Harmondsworth, 1978.
54. CW VII, p.361.
55. *The Journals of Anaïs Nin, 1931–1934*, p.234.
56. CW IV, p.84.
57. Ibid, p.85.
58. CW III, p.83.
59. CW IV, p.73.
60. Ibid, p.75.
61. Ibid, p.77.
62. CW II, p.287.
63. Letter to Jeanne Ridel, CW III, p.291.
64. 'Appeal to Youth, Intoxication – Detoxification', CW VIII, p.20.

65. CW III, p.298.
66. Letter to André Gide, CW V, p.176.
67. CW IV, p.196.
68. Blin, *Souvenirs et propos*, p.28.
69. *The Cenci* (text written for *La Bête Noire*), CW V, pp.36–7.
70. CW V, pp.226–7.
71. Ibid, p.188.

Chapter 3: Mexico, Brussels, Ireland

1. 'A Note on Peyote' (1947), CW IX, 1979, p.97.
2. 'An Affective Athleticism', CW IV, p.132.
3. CW IV, pp.143–4.
4. Ibid, p.14.
5. CW V, p.190.
6. 'The Awakening of the Thunderbird', CW VIII, 1980, p.414.
7. 'Mexico and Civilization', ibid, pp.129–30.
8. CW VIII, p.283.
9. Letter to Dr Allendy, ibid, p.207.
10. CW V, pp.196–7.
11. 'The Race of Lost Men', CW IX, p.79.
12. CW V, p.198.
13. CW VIII, p.313.
14. Letter to René Thomas, ibid, p.310.
15. 'And it was in Mexico' (1947) in *The Tarahumaras*, L'Arbalète, Décines, 1963, p.128.
16. 'The Peyote Dance', CW IX, p.41.
17. Ibid, p.40.
18. 'And it was in Mexico', p.121.
19. 'Tutuguri' (1948), CW IX, p.55.
20. CW VII, p.161.
21. CW IX, p.80.
22. CW VII, pp.191–2.
23. Ibid, pp.119–21.
24. Ibid, p.144.
25. Ibid, p.202.
26. Ibid, p.202.
27. Ibid, p.204.
28. Letter to Anne Manson, CW VII, p.215.
29. CW VII, p.206.
30. Ibid, p.214.
31. Letter to André Breton, CW VII, p.212.
32. CW VII, p.215.
33. Ibid, p.228.
34. Letter to André Breton, CW VII, p.224.
35. 'And it was in Mexico', p.126.
36. Letter to Henri Parisot in *Letters from Rodez*, CW IX, p.177.
37. Letter to Arthur Adamov, CW XI, 1974, pp.62–3.

Chapter 4: Years of Incarceration

1. Letter to Jean Paulhan (23 March 1946), CW XI, p.212.
2. Artaud's friend Paule Thévenin believes that Artaud wrote no letters from Sainte-Anne. It is conceivable that Roger Blin was thinking of the letters which he received from the asylum of Ville-Évrard.
3. Blin, *Souvenirs et propos*, p.30.
4. Letter to Anne Manson (27 December 1943), CW X, 1974, pp.157–8.
5. *Lettres à Anie Besnard*, p.7.
6. Ibid, p.7.
7. Ibid, p.10.
8. *Nouveaux Écrits de Rodez*, Gallimard, Paris, 1977, pp.28–9.
9. 'Spell' reproduced in *Antonin Artaud, Dessins et portraits*, pp.138–9.
10. Ibid, pp.136–7.
11. Ibid, p.26.
12. *Antonin Artaud, dessins*, CGP, Paris, 1987, p.8.
13. Ibid, p.8.
14. Interview with the author, Paris, March 1987.
15. Card to René Thomas, *Antonin Artaud, dessins*, p.8.
16. *Nouveaux Écrits de Rodez*, p.54.
17. Ferdière, 'I treated Antonin Artaud' in *La Tour de Feu* nos. 63/64, Jarnac, 1959, p.35.
18. *Convulsive Therapy, Theory and Practice*, Raven Press, New York, 1979, p.159.
19. Interview with the author, Aubervilliers, March 1987.
20. *Nouveaux Écrits de Rodez*, p.40.
21. Ibid, p.59.
22. Letter to Jean Paulhan, CW X, p.105.
23. Letter to Gaston Ferdière, *Nouveaux Écrits de Rodez*, p.50.
24. Letter to Roger Blin, CW XI, p.120.
25. CW X, p.104.
26. *Nouveaux Écrits de Rodez*, p.127.
27. Interview with the author, Paris, March 1987.
28. 'And it was in Mexico', p.125.
29. Interview with the author, Paris, March 1987.
30. Ibid.
31. Dequeker, 'The Extermination of Proprieties' (1950) collected in *Artaud Vivant* (ed. O. Virmaux), Oswald, Paris, 1980, pp.155–6.
32. CW XVIII, 1983, p.108.
33. Letter to Gaston Gallimard, CW XI, p.38.
34. Introduction (1970, trans. Richard Howard) to *Soledad Brother: The Prison Letters of George Jackson*, Penguin, Harmondsworth, 1971, p.18.
35. CW XI, p.149.
36. CW XIV*, 1978, p.148.
37. Letter to Henri Thomas, CW XIV*, p.48.
38. *Letters from Rodez*, CW IX, p.169.
39. Ibid, p.171.
40. Letter to Arthur Adamov, CW XIV*, p.94.
41. CW XI, p.177.

42. CW XIV*, p.76.
43. Ibid, p.84.
44. Letter to Colette Thomas, CW XIV*, p.84.
45. Interview with Paule Thévenin by the author, Paris, April 1987.
46. Colette Thomas, *The Testament of the Dead Daughter*, Gallimard, Paris, 1954, p.151.
47. Letter to Colette Thomas, CW XIV*, p.107.
48. CW XI, p.205.
49. CW XI, p.216.
50. CW XIV*, p.21.
51. Letter to Jean Paulhan, CW XI, p.278.

Chapter 5: Ivry – Blows and Bombs

1. Prevel, *En Compagnie d'Antonin Artaud*, p.14.
2. Henri Thomas, 'Présentation' in *Magazine Littéraire* no. 206, Paris, 1984, p.17.
3. *L'Éphémère* no. 8, p.49.
4. Blin, *Souvenirs et propos*, p.34.
5. Isou, 'Nouvelle Préface' (1982, inserted typescript) to *Antonin Artaud torturé par les psychiatres*.
6. *En Compagnie d'Antonin Artaud*, p.56.
7. Ibid, p.64.
8. Ibid, p.120.
9. CW XXII, 1986, p.67.
10. 'The Execration of the Father–Mother' in *Artaud the Mômo*, CW XII, 1974, p.39.
11. Unpublished letter of 6 February 1947.
12. CW I*, p.11.
13. *Lettres à Anie Besnard*, p.49.
14. CW XIV*, p.26.
15. Ibid, p.30.
16. CW XXIV, 1988, p.66.
17. *Interjections*, CW XIV**, 1978, p.154.
18. CW XIV**, p.234.
19. *K* nos. 1/2, Paris, 1948, p.108.
20. *L'Éphémére*, pp.4–5.
21. Ibid, p.22.
22. Ibid, p.4.
23. Ibid, pp.20–1.
24. Ibid, p.6.
25. CW XIII, 1974, p.54.
26. Ibid, pp.15.
27. Ibid, pp.38.
28. Ibid, p.17.
29. *En Compagnie d'Antonin Artaud*, p.137.
30. Ibid, p.139.
31. *Les Lettres Nouvelles* no. 59, Paris, 1958, p.481.

32. *Antonin Artaud, dessins*, p.24.
33. Ibid, p.22.
34. Ibid, p.48.
35. Ibid, p.49.
36. *L'Arbalète* no. 13, Décines, 1948, p.7.
37. *En Compagnie d'Antonin Artaud*, p.151.
38. *L'Arbalète*, pp.15–16.
39. *En Compagnie d'Antonin Artaud*, p.154.
40. *Artaud Vivant*, p.220.
41. That is, at the Vieux-Colombier.
42. *En Compagnie d'Antonin Artaud*, p.155.
43. *L'Arbalète*, p.24.
44. *En Compagnie d'Antonin Artaud*, p.156.
45. *L'Arve et l'Aume suivi de 24 lettres à Marc Barbezat*, L'Arbalète, Décines, 1989, p.82.
46. *En Compagnie d'Antonin Artaud*, p.173.
47. *84* nos. 8/9, Paris, 1949, p.282.
48. Ibid, p.284.
49. *La Nouvelle Revue Française* (new series) issue 89, Paris, 1960, p.1017.
50. *Combat*, Paris, 1 November 1947, p.2.
51. CW XIII, p.233.
52. Ibid, p.116.
53. Ibid, pp.258–9.
54. Ibid, p.273.
55. Interview with Paule Thévenin by the author, Paris, April 1987.
56. Casarès, *Résidente Privilégiée*, Fayard, Paris, 1980, p.468.
57. CW XIII, p.84.
58. Ibid, pp.91–2.
59. Ibid, p.233.
60. 'The Theatre of Cruelty' (1947), CW XIII, p.110.
61. *L'Arve et l'Aume suivi de 24 lettres à Marc Barbezat*, p.93.
62. *84* nos. 5/6, Paris, 1948, p.136.
63. Extract in *Antonin Artaud, Dessins et portraits*, p.47.
64. Reported by Paule Thévenin in 'Antonin Artaud dans la vie', in *Tel Quel* no. 20, Paris, 1965, p.33.
65. Interview with the author, Paris, July 1987.
66. CW XIII, p.130.
67. Ibid, pp.136–7.
68. Ibid, p.139.
69. 'Préface' to *Nouveaux Écrits de Rodez*, p.8.
70. 'The beings do not emerge in the outside day' in *84* nos. 5/6, p.100.
71. Unpublished letter of 14 February 1948.
72. CW IX, p.58.
73. *L'Arve et l'Aume suivi de 24 lettres à Marc Barbezat*, p.97.
74. Letter to Paule Thévenin (24 February 1948), CW XIII, p.146.
75. Ibid, pp.146–7.
76. *Combat*, Paris, 5 March 1948, p.2.
77. Ibid, p.2.

78. *Le Figaro Littéraire*, Paris, 13 March 1948, p.3.
79. Ibid, p.3.
80. Ibid, p.3.
81. *Antonin Artaud, dessins*, p.16.
82. Adamov, *L'Homme et l'Enfant*, Gallimard, Paris, 1968, p.83.

Bibliography and Filmography

Books by Artaud in French

Collected Works (*Oeuvres complètes*), Gallimard, Paris, 1956– ; revised edition
    1976– , edited by Paule Thévenin.
    Volume I contains: *Correspondence with Jacques Rivière*, early poetry, Surrealist
        poetry, reworked Surrealist open letters, Surrealist texts and letters.
    II: Texts and photographs around the Alfred Jarry Theatre, reviews, letters.
    III: Film scenarios, film writings, letters and photographs.
    IV: *The Theatre and its Double* and *The Cenci*.
    V: Texts and letters around *The Theatre and its Double* and *The Cenci*.
    VI: Adaptation of Matthew Gregory Lewis's novel *The Monk*, photographs,
        letters.
    VII: *Heliogabalus* and *The New Revelations of Being*, letters (including those sent
        from Ireland).
    VIII: Diverse texts, letters and journalism, *Revolutionary Messages*.
    IX: *The Tarahumaras* and *Letters from Rodez*, texts from the Rodez period.
    X: Letters written at Rodez, 1943–4.
    XI: Letters written at Rodez, 1945–6.
    XII: *Artaud the Mômo* (including drawings) and *Here Lies preceded by The Indian
        Culture*.
    XIII: *Van Gogh the Suicide of society* and *To have done with the judgement of god*,
        documents, letters.
    XIV: *Henchmen and Torturings*.
    XV: Exercise books from Rodez, February–April 1945.
    XVI: Exercise books from Rodez, May–June 1945.
    XVII: Exercise books from Rodez, July–August 1945.
    XVIII: Exercise books from Rodez, September–November 1945.
    XIX: Exercise books from Rodez, December 1945–January 1946.
    XX: Exercise books from Rodez, February–March 1946.
    XXI: Exercise books from Rodez, April–25 May 1946.
    XXII: Exercise books from Paris, 26 May–July 1946.
    XXIII: Exercise books from Paris, August–September 1946.
    XXIV: Exercise books from Paris, October–November 1946.
    XXV: Exercise books from Paris, December 1946–January 1947.
Nouveaux Écrits de Rodez, Gallimard, Paris, 1977: Texts, letters and photographs
    from the Rodez period.
Lettres à Génica Athanasiou, Gallimard, Paris, 1969: Letters from 1921 to 1940.
Lettres à Anie Besnard, Le Nouveau Commerce, Paris, 1977: Letters from 1941 to
    1947.

L'Arve et l'Aume suivi de 24 lettres à Marc Barbezat, L'Arbalète, Décines, 1989:
  Text from 1943 (revised in 1947), letters from 1947 and 1948.
Van Gogh the Suicide of society, Gallimard, Paris, 1990: Deluxe edition of text from
  1947, including colour reproductions of the paintings Artaud deals with in the
  text.
The Vieux-Colombier Lecture, in *L'Infini*, no. 34, Paris, 1991: Text which Artaud
  prepared for his performance at the Vieux-Colombier Theatre in Paris on 13
  January 1947, but then abandoned in favour of an improvisation.

Books by Artaud in English

Artaud Anthology (ed. Jack Hirschmann), City Lights, San Francisco, 1965.
Antonin Artaud: Selected Writings (ed. and with an introduction by Susan Sontag),
  Farrar, Straus and Giroux, New York, 1976. [This and the above anthology are
  both excellent; Hirschmann's collection suffers from weak translations and a
  poor sense of chronology.]
The Peyote Dance, Farrar, Straus and Giroux, New York, 1976.
The Theatre and its Double, Calder, London, 1977.
Collected Works (Volumes 1 to 4), Calder, London, 1968–74. [Dire translations.]
Artaud on Theatre (ed. Claude Schumacher), Methuen, London, 1990. [An
  unadventurous collection with a banal commentary and weak translations.]

Drawings by Artaud

None of Artaud's drawings is on permanent display. Three catalogues of the
  drawings have been published.

Antonin Artaud, Dessins et portraits, Gallimard, Paris, 1986. [A beautiful catalogue
  which reproduces almost all of Artaud's drawings, and also some exercise book
  pages featuring drawings and texts. To be published in an English-language
  version by Abbeville Press, New York.]

Antonin Artaud, dessins, CGP, Paris, 1987. [The catalogue of the excellent
  exhibition of Artaud's drawings at the Centre Georges Pompidou in Paris in
  1987.]

Antonin Artaud (1896–1948), Dessins, Musée de l'Abbaye Sainte-Croix, Les Sables
  d'Olonne, 1980. [The catalogue of a smaller exhibition of Artaud's drawings at
  the Musée de l'Abbaye Sainte-Croix in Les Sables d'Olonne in 1980.]

Recordings by Artaud

Les Malades et les médecins (The Patients and the doctors), 8 June 1946.
Aliénation et magie noire (Madness and black magic), 16 July 1946. [Both of these
  recordings for radio can be heard at the Audio-Visual Archive of the
  Bibliothèque Gaston Baty in Paris.]
Pour en finir avec le jugement de dieu (To have done with the judgement of god), 22
  November 1947 to 16 January 1948. [A record of this work for radio, banned in
  February 1948 and not transmitted, was released on the Harmonia Mundi label
  in November 1986.]

Films with Acting Appearances by Artaud

1924: *Fait Divers*, dir. Claude Autant-Lara
Surcouf, dir. Luitz-Morat
1925: *Graziella*, dir. Marcel Vandal
1926: *Le Juif Errant*, dir. Luitz-Morat
Napoléon, dir. Abel Gance (silent version)
Mathusalem, dir. Jean Painlevé and René Sti
1927: *Verdun, Souvenirs d'Histoire*, dir. Léon Poirier
La Passion de Jeanne d'Arc, dir. Carl Theodor Dreyer
1928: *L'Argent*, dir. Marcel L'Herbier
1929: *Tarakanova*, dir. Raymond Bernard
1930: *La Femme d'une Nuit*, dir. Marcel L'Herbier
L'Opéra de quat'sous, dir. G. W. Pabst [Artaud appears only in the French
language version of the film]
1931: *Faubourg Montmartre*, dir. Raymond Bernard
Verdun, Souvenirs d'Histoire, dir Léon Poirier (re-shot sound version)
Les Croix de Bois, dir. Raymond Bernard
1932: *Coup de Feu à l'Aube*, dir. Serge Poligny
Mater Dolorosa, dir. Abel Gance
L'Enfant de ma Soeur, dir. Henri Wulschleger
1933: *Liliom*, dir. Fritz Lang
1934: *Sidonie Panache*, dir. Henri Wulschleger
Napoléon, dir. Abel Gance (re-cut sound version)
1935: *Lucrèce Borgia*, dir. Abel Gance
Koenigsmark, dir. Maurice Tourneur

Film with Scenario Written by Artaud

1927: *La Coquille et le Clergyman*, dir. Germaine Dulac

Index